COOKING IN «

SEASON

with

THE FRESH MARKET

PHOTOGRAPHS BY JENNIFER DAVICK

CHRONICLE BOOKS

SAN FRANCISCO

Published exclusively for The Fresh Market, Inc. by Chronicle Books LLC.

ISBN: 978-1-4521-1978-6

Manufactured in the United States of America.

Art direction by Alex Blake
Design by Stitch Design Co.
Food styling by Marian Cooper Cairns
Prop styling by Amy Wilson
Text by Rick Rodgers

This book has been set in Sentinel, Gotham, and Cactus.

10 9 8 7 6 5 4 3 2 1

Chronicle Books LLC
680 Second Street
San Francisco, CA 94107
www.chroniclebooks.com/custom

>-‹‹

SPRING

SUMMER

FALL

WINTER

DF ‖ DAIRY-FREE   GF ‖ GLUTEN-FREE   ∨ ‖ VEGAN   ∪ ‖ VEGETARIAN   🍷 ‖ WINE   🍺 ‖ BEER

INTRODUCTION

The current convenience of buying the produce we want when we want it is a new one, really less than one hundred years old.

For eons, humans relied on fruits and vegetables that were planted, grown, and harvested locally and according to the seasons, often by farmers whom they knew. Livestock, too, was raised at specific times of year. Waiting for the annual bounty to arrive was akin to anticipating a wonderful gift. Spring's sweet strawberries, colorful summer tomatoes, tangy autumn cranberries, and satisfyingly earthy winter squash—these are just a few of the foods that are still synonymous with the traditional harvesting cycles.

Today, the sheer number of people in the world has changed our farming methods. We are no longer constrained by the seasons. We are blessed with an abundance and variety of foods that can be sourced from all around the world. But cooking with the seasons reaffirms the natural progression of life, and guarantees food that is at the peak of flavor and freshness.

At The Fresh Market, we celebrate great food. That is why we strive to have local, sustainable produce available throughout the year. We enjoy the convenience of year-round availability, but we value the time-honored experience of being renewed by the changing seasons. Biting into that first juicy peach is just as much a summer icon as jumping into a cool stream on a hot afternoon.

Cooking in Season with The Fresh Market is a cookbook built around food at the peak of its seasonal perfection. We've created ninety recipes that deliver maximum flavor with a minimum amount of effort, letting the fresh ingredients shine. We've included recipes for holidays and special events, from pulled pork for a backyard barbecue to a showstopping roast turkey with gravy. If you have specific dietary needs, you'll find recipes marked as vegetarian, vegan, dairy-free, and gluten-free. The recipes are divided into the quarterly seasons, and within each season are grouped by course. Many include wine or beer recommendations.

In other words, we have tried to make this cookbook as useful as possible and to anticipate your needs as a busy cook. Customer satisfaction is a way of life at The Fresh Market and has been ever since Ray and Beverly Berry opened our first store in Greensboro, North Carolina, focused on providing both exceptional food and exceptional customer service. Inspired by the foodmarkets of Europe, we offer an intimate, personalized shopping experience where you can handpick meat and seafood with the assistance of our butcher and fishmonger; carefully choose your produce; or slow down and sip a cup of freshly brewed coffee. We offer the international specialty items that you may not easily find elsewhere, with ingredients for Indian, Mexican, Asian, and other cuisines. Many foods are sold in bulk, so you can buy just as much as you need.

Our commitment to freshness is obvious in our name. The basis of our business is perishable goods, which will be sold only if the quality is high and the freshness is apparent. When we opened our doors thirty years ago, our kind of market— offering an inviting and relaxing environment—was a new concept. As we continue to open stores to serve new communities, we attract customers who like our great-tasting products and enjoyable shopping experience.

Our motto at The Fresh Market is "Experience the Food!" By using *Cooking in Season with The Fresh Market*, you will be able to do just that, embracing the naturally occurring cycles that all humans need to sustain themselves . . . deliciously.

MENU
BUILDER

APPETIZERS
DF 🌱 🍴 Giant Artichokes with Mustard-Herb Vinaigrette 11
🍴 Deviled Eggs with Fresh Horseradish 13

SOUP & SALADS
DF GF 🌱 🍴 Roasted Beet Salad with Watercress & Tomatoes 14
DF Pan-Asian Noodle Soup with Bok Choy 15
DF 🌱 🍴 Radish Tabbouleh 17
DF GF 🌱 🍴 Sugar Snap Peas with Tarragon Vinaigrette 19

MAIN COURSES
DF Roast Leg of Lamb with Mint Aioli 21
DF GF Chicken Legs with Vidalia Onion Gravy 22
DF Beef Stew with Stout 23
DF Italian Stir-Fry with Beef & Spring Vegetables 24
DF Oven-Poached Salmon Fillets with Watercress Mayonnaise 27
DF Scallops & Snow Peas with Ginger 29
DF Fish Tacos with Mango Salsa 33

PASTA & SIDE DISHES
🍴 Braised Radishes with Green Onions 35
🍴 Fettuccine with Asparagus & Ricotta 37
GF 🍴 Asparagus with Gremolata Butter 38
Steakhouse Creamed Spinach 40

DESSERTS
🍴 Key Lime Cheesecake 41
🍴 Mango Cashew Crisp 43
GF 🍴 Almond Meringues with Strawberry Compote 45
GF 🍴 Vanilla Ice Cream with Rhubarb Sauce 47
🍴 Strawberry Tart with Mascarpone Filling 49

DF ‖ DAIRY-FREE   GF ‖ GLUTEN-FREE   🌱 ‖ VEGAN   🍴 ‖ VEGETARIAN

SPRING

SPRING IS THE SEASON THAT

CARRIES THE PROMISE OF DELICIOUS EATING IN THE COMING YEAR.

The first perennial herbs, such as tarragon and chives, peek through the soil, ready to season radishes, beets, and snow peas, along with other spring vegetables, such as tender stalks of asparagus and firm artichokes. Strawberries are perhaps the most iconic spring fruit, but exotic mangoes and tart Key limes also make an appearance. The spring holidays of Easter and Passover celebrate renewal with menus that feature the traditional foods of the season.

GIANT ARTICHOKES

with MUSTARD-HERB VINAIGRETTE

When extra-large, softball-sized artichokes arrive in late spring, they can be simmered to tenderness and served with a vinaigrette as a light lunch. As you work your way through the artichoke, your reward is the wide, saucer-shaped flesh at the base. Tying the artichokes with kitchen twine helps them keep their shape for serving, and the lemon slices impart flavor.

YOU WILL NEED

$1/2$ teaspoon black peppercorns

2 lemons

$1/4$ cup distilled white or cider vinegar

4 very large artichokes (about 12 ounces each), stemmed

VINAIGRETTE

Grated zest of 1 lemon

2 tablespoons fresh lemon juice

2 tablespoons red wine vinegar

1 teaspoon Dijon mustard

1 garlic clove, crushed and peeled

1 cup extra-virgin olive oil

2 teaspoons minced fresh chives

2 teaspoons minced fresh tarragon

2 teaspoons minced fresh flat-leaf parsley

Kosher salt and freshly ground black pepper

1 Bring a large stockpot of salted water, with peppercorns, to a boil over high heat.

2 Cut eight $1/4$-inch-thick rounds from lemons; set aside. Pour vinegar into a large nonreactive bowl and half-fill with cold water.

3 Using a large, sharp knife, one at a time cut off top inch from each artichoke. Using scissors, snip off thorny tips from artichoke leaves. Put each trimmed artichoke in vinegar water to discourage browning while preparing remaining artichokes.

4 Drain artichokes, discarding vinegar water. Sit an artichoke on a lemon slice and place a second lemon slice on top. Using kitchen twine, tie artichoke and lemon slices like a package to hold lemon slices in place.

continued

5 Add artichokes to boiling water and partially cover with a lid. Reduce heat to medium. Cook at a brisk simmer, occasionally turning artichokes, until a bottom leaf can be easily pulled from a base and flesh is tender (scrape leaf against your teeth to check), about 1 1/4 hours. Using tongs, transfer artichokes, upside down, to a platter to drain. Let cool. (Artichokes can be covered with plastic wrap and refrigerated for up to 1 day.)

6 To make vinaigrette: Pulse lemon zest and juice, vinegar, mustard, and garlic in a blender to combine. With machine running, gradually pour oil through hole in lid to emulsify. Add chives, tarragon, and parsley and pulse to combine without puréeing herbs. Season with salt and pepper. (Vinaigrette can be made up to 2 hours ahead. If separated, pulse a few times to re-emulsify.) Pour vinaigrette into 4 ramekins.

7 Gently squeeze each artichoke to remove excess water. Remove twine and lemon slices. Serve each artichoke in a shallow soup bowl with a ramekin of vinaigrette for dipping and a large bowl to collect leaves.

ARTICHOKES

The first human to eat an artichoke must have been very intrepid, very hungry, or both. It had to have been quite a process to figure out how to scrape the tender flesh from the leaves and eventually reach the meaty heart. In fact, not all of the heart is edible, and the bitter, feathery center must be removed before saving the delicious artichoke heart. Cooking must have come into play, too, because raw artichokes aren't too tasty. The edible part is actually the bud of a thorny thistle plant.

Virtually all commercially grown American artichokes come from the area around Castroville, California, simply because the region has the necessary growing climate of warm days and cool nights. The season peaks in April and May, and you'll find artichokes ranging in size from baby to giant, with most weighing in at about six ounces. Boiling is the most familiar way to cook artichokes (especially for the very large ones), but they can also be steamed, roasted, and even grilled. Store artichokes, uncovered, in the refrigerator for up to three days before cooking.

· DEVILED EGGS ·

with FRESH HORSERADISH

APPETIZER

MAKES 4–8 SERVINGS

Fresh horseradish is an eye-opening seasoning and a delicious substitution for the bottled version. Here, it adds zest to what can be a stodgy classic. While you may have your own method of boiling eggs, try our technique, which prevents cracking and discolored yolks.

YOU WILL NEED

8 large eggs

¼ cup mayonnaise

2 tablespoons freshly grated horseradish (see note), plus more for garnish

1 tablespoon heavy cream or milk

Kosher salt and freshly ground black pepper

Minced fresh flat-leaf parsley or chives, for garnish (optional)

1 Put eggs in a medium saucepan and add cold water to cover. Bring just to a boil over high heat. Remove saucepan from heat and cover tightly. Let stand for 12 minutes. Pour out hot water from saucepan and replace it with ice water. Let eggs stand until chilled, about 10 minutes. Crack eggs. Starting at larger end of each egg, and working under a thin stream of cold running water, remove shells.

2 Cut each egg in half lengthwise and remove yolk. Using a rubber spatula, rub yolks through a sieve into a bowl. Stir in mayonnaise, 2 tablespoons horseradish, and cream and season with salt and pepper. Use a small spoon to stuff egg whites with filling. (For a professional look, transfer yolk mixture to a pastry bag fitted with a star tip. Pipe yolk mixture into whites.) Place on a serving platter, cover loosely with plastic wrap, and refrigerate until serving, up to 8 hours.

3 To serve, grate a little more horseradish on top of each egg and sprinkle with parsley, if using. Serve chilled.

HORSERADISH: To prepare fresh horseradish, pare away the thick tan peel with a sharp knife and grate the white flesh with a Microplane zester with moderately large holes or the small holes of a box grater. Grate any leftover root and place in a covered jar. Pour in enough cider vinegar or distilled white vinegar to cover the root. Refrigerated, horseradish root will keep this way for two months.

ROASTED BEET SALAD

with WATERCRESS & TOMATOES

SALAD

MAKES 6 SERVINGS

We usually think of cooking beets by boiling them, but roasting is a much more flavorful method that has turned many beet haters into beet lovers. Use beets of a similar size so they cook evenly.

YOU WILL NEED

6 unpeeled beets (about 1 ½ pounds), scrubbed

2 tablespoons sherry vinegar or red wine vinegar

Kosher salt and freshly ground black pepper

½ cup extra-virgin olive oil

1 cup grape or cherry tomatoes, halved lengthwise

1 small red onion, halved and sliced into thin half-moons

2 bunches watercress (about 8 ounces total), stemmed

1 Preheat oven to 400°F. Wrap each beet in aluminum foil and place on a rimmed baking sheet. Bake until beets are barely tender when pierced with a small, sharp knife, about 1 hour. Let cool until easy to handle. Slip off beet skins. Halve beets and cut into ½-inch-thick half-moons.

2 Whisk vinegar, ½ teaspoon salt, and ¼ teaspoon pepper in a medium bowl. Gradually whisk in oil. Add beets, tomatoes, and red onion and toss well. (Salad can be made to this point up to 1 hour ahead, or refrigerated for up to 8 hours.)

3 Just before serving, add watercress and toss again. Reseason with salt and pepper. Serve at room temperature or chilled.

PAN-ASIAN

NOODLE SOUP

with BOK CHOY

SOUP

MAKES 4 SERVINGS

WINE SUGGESTION: BEAUJOLAIS

This recipe borrows seasonings from several Asian cuisines. Bok choy, with its mild cabbage flavor, is the main vegetable here, but you could substitute asparagus or sugar snap peas. Mai fun, also called cellophane noodles or bean threads, are made from soybeans.

YOU WILL NEED

2 ounces mai fun

12 ounces boneless beef sirloin steak, trimmed of excess fat

2 tablespoons vegetable oil

$1/2$ cup thinly sliced shallots

2 tablespoons shredded fresh ginger

2 garlic cloves, minced

1 head bok choy ($1 1/4$ pounds), cut crosswise into $1/4$-inch-wide slices

2 cups reduced-sodium chicken broth

2 cups water

2 tablespoons Chinese rice wine or dry sherry

2 tablespoons Japanese soy sauce

1 tablespoon light brown sugar

$1/2$ teaspoon Sriracha or other red pepper sauce

Fresh cilantro leaves and lime wedges for serving

1 Place mai fun in a small bowl, add enough very hot water to cover and set aside. Holding knife at a 45-degree angle, cut steak across grain into wide, thin slices. Cut slices crosswise into pieces about 3 inches long.

2 Heat 1 tablespoon of oil in a large, heavy wok or sauté pan over high heat until very hot. In batches, without crowding, add beef and cook, stirring occasionally, until it loses its pink color, about $1 1/2$ minutes. Transfer to a plate.

3 Add remaining 1 tablespoon oil to saucepan. Add shallots, ginger, and garlic and stir-fry until shallot softens, about 1 minute. Add bok choy and stir-fry until wilted, about 2 minutes. Add broth, water, rice wine, soy sauce, brown sugar, and Sriracha and bring to a boil. Drain mai fun and return to bowl. Using kitchen scissors, snip through mai fun a few times to make shorter lengths. Stir beef and mai fun into soup. Ladle into deep soup bowls, sprinkle with cilantro, and serve hot with lime wedges.

RADISH TABBOULEH

SALAD

MAKES 6 SERVINGS

Bulgur wheat is parboiled and cracked wheat kernels, not a particular grain variety. Soaking is the best way to soften bulgur, and then it takes just a few minutes to turn it into tabbouleh, a versatile salad that can be part of an outdoor picnic or a side dish for grilled meats and fish. Radishes add color and spicy flavor to the standard recipe. To make a few more servings, shred the lettuce and stir it into the tabbouleh.

YOU WILL NEED

1 cup medium-grain bulgur wheat

1 $^3/_4$ cups boiling water

2 tablespoons fresh lemon juice

Kosher salt and freshly ground black pepper

$^1/_2$ cup extra-virgin olive oil

1 bunch (about 10) radishes, trimmed and thinly sliced

$^1/_3$ cup minced fresh flat-leaf parsley

2 green onions, including green parts, thinly sliced

1 romaine lettuce heart, separated into individual leaves

1 Combine bulgur and boiling water in a medium bowl. Stir well and let stand until bulgur is tender, about 45 minutes. Drain well in a wire sieve, pressing hard on bulgur with a large spoon to remove any excess liquid.

2 Whisk together lemon juice, $^1/_2$ teaspoon salt, and $^1/_4$ teaspoon pepper in a medium bowl. Gradually whisk in oil. Add bulgur, radishes, parsley, and green onions and mix well. Cover and refrigerate for at least 1 hour before serving.

3 Season tabbouleh with salt and pepper (grain salads tend to need seasoning again after soaking up dressing). Line a serving platter with romaine leaves and heap the tabbouleh on top. Serve chilled or at room temperature, using the leaves to scoop up and eat the tabbouleh, if desired.

SUGAR SNAP PEAS

SALAD

DF | GF | 🍸 | 🔱

with TARRAGON VINAIGRETTE

MAKES 6 SERVINGS

This very simple salad, which can also serve as a side dish for grilled salmon, is proof that when your ingredients are top-notch, you don't need to do much to them to create a satisfying dish. For a lovely variation, sprinkle the salad with some crumbled goat cheese.

YOU WILL NEED

12 ounces sugar snap peas, trimmed

1 lemon

¹/₄ teaspoon salt

A few grinds of black pepper

¹/₄ cup extra-virgin olive oil

2 tablespoons minced fresh tarragon

1 Bring a medium saucepan of lightly salted water to a boil over high heat. Add sugar snap peas and cook just until crisp-tender, about 3 minutes. Drain in a colander, rinse under cold running water, and drain well. Pat dry with paper towels.

2 Grate zest from lemon onto a plate and set aside. Squeeze 1 tablespoon lemon juice and transfer to a medium bowl. Save remaining lemon for another use. Add salt and pepper to lemon juice and gradually whisk in oil. Stir in tarragon. Add sugar snap peas and stir gently.

3 Transfer to a serving bowl and sprinkle with lemon zest. Serve now or refrigerate for up to 2 hours if not serving immediately.

ROAST LEG OF LAMB

with MINT AIOLI

MAIN COURSE

MAKES 8 SERVINGS

WINE SUGGESTION: OREGON PINOT NOIR

For many cooks, leg of lamb is the preferred main course for Easter dinner. Here's one of the easiest and best ways to roast boneless leg of lamb, with a mint-and-garlic mayonnaise as an easy sauce.

YOU WILL NEED

AIOLI

1 ¼ cups mayonnaise

3 tablespoons minced fresh mint

2 garlic cloves, crushed through a garlic press

One 4 ½-pound boneless leg of lamb, excess fat trimmed

½ teaspoon kosher salt

¼ teaspoon freshly ground black pepper

Fresh mint sprigs for garnish (optional)

1. To make aioli: Stir aioli ingredients together in a small bowl. Cover and refrigerate for at least 1 hour or up to 1 day.

2. Preheat oven to 450°F.

3. Season lamb with salt and pepper. Place lamb, smooth side up, on a rimmed baking sheet or in a shallow roasting pan. Let stand at room temperature for 30 minutes.

4. Roast lamb until an instant-read thermometer inserted in thickest part of lamb reads 125°F for medium-rare, about 45 minutes. Transfer lamb to a carving board and let stand for 10 minutes.

5. Using a sharp, thin knife, cut meat across grain into slices and transfer to a serving platter. Pour any carving juices over lamb. Garnish with mint sprigs, if using, and serve hot, with mint aioli.

· CHICKEN LEGS ·

MAIN COURSE

with VIDALIA ONION GRAVY

MAKES 4 SERVINGS

WINE SUGGESTION: SPANISH ROSÉ

Vidalia onions, which hail from Georgia, start their season in late spring. Much mellower and sweeter than yellow onions, here they are baked with chicken and turned into a luscious gravy. Serve this dish with mashed potatoes or biscuits. Use vegetable broth to make this recipe gluten-free.

YOU WILL NEED

2 Vidalia or other large sweet onions (1 $\frac{1}{2}$ pounds), cut lengthwise into quarters

2 tablespoons extra-virgin olive oil

Kosher salt and freshly ground black pepper

Four 12-ounce chicken legs

1 $\frac{1}{2}$ teaspoons minced fresh thyme, plus fresh thyme sprigs for garnish

$\frac{1}{4}$ cup dry white vermouth or dry white wine

$\frac{3}{4}$ cup reduced-sodium chicken or vegetable broth

1 Preheat oven to 425°F. Lightly oil a large roasting pan. Toss onion quarters with 1 tablespoon of oil, $\frac{1}{2}$ teaspoon salt, and $\frac{1}{4}$ teaspoon pepper in roasting pan. Roast for 10 minutes.

2 Remove pan from oven. Arrange chicken on top of onions and brush with remaining 1 tablespoon oil. Season with 1 teaspoon salt and $\frac{1}{2}$ teaspoon pepper. Sprinkle minced thyme over chicken and onions. Return pan to oven and roast, occasionally stirring onions, including those under chicken, until chicken is golden brown and an instant-read thermometer inserted in a thigh registers 165°F, 35 to 40 minutes. Transfer chicken to a platter and tent with aluminum foil. If onions aren't caramelized, increase oven temperature to 475°F and continue roasting until they are deep golden brown, about 5 minutes longer.

3 Transfer onions and any pan juices to a food processor or blender. Place roasting pan over medium-high heat. Add vermouth and bring to a boil, scraping up browned bits in bottom of pan with a wooden spoon. Stir in broth. Boil until reduced to $\frac{2}{3}$ cup, about 2 minutes. Purée onions, adding broth mixture as needed to make a smooth sauce. Season with salt and pepper. Spoon sauce over chicken, garnish with thyme sprigs, and serve hot.

BEEF STEW WITH STOUT

BEER SUGGESTION: IRISH STOUT

St. Patrick's Day is officially in winter, but is close enough to the vernal equinox to qualify as a spring holiday. Irish stout, with its dark color and robust flavor, adds a deep flavor to this stew, which could be served with buttered steamed cabbage.

YOU WILL NEED

3 tablespoons vegetable oil

2 1/2 pounds beef sirloin tips, trimmed of fat and cut into 1-inch cubes

Kosher salt and freshly ground black pepper

1 yellow onion, chopped

10 ounces white mushrooms, sliced

1/4 cup all-purpose flour

2 tablespoons tomato paste

1 tablespoon light brown sugar

6 garlic cloves, minced

2 cups reduced-sodium beef broth

One 11.2-ounce bottle Irish stout, such as Guinness

8 ounces baby carrots

2 large baking (russet) potatoes, peeled and cut into 1-inch dice

1 Preheat oven to 300°F. Heat 2 tablespoons of oil in a Dutch oven or heavy-bottomed flameproof casserole over medium heat. Season beef with 1 teaspoon salt and 1/2 teaspoon pepper. In batches, add beef to pot and cook, turning occasionally, until browned on all sides, about 6 minutes. Transfer beef to a plate.

2 Add remaining 1 tablespoon oil to pot. Add onion and cook over medium heat, stirring, until softened, about 3 minutes. Add mushrooms and cook, stirring occasionally, until their juices evaporate and mushrooms begin to brown, 7 to 10 minutes. Sprinkle with flour and stir well. Add tomato paste, brown sugar, and garlic and cook for 1 minute, stirring with a wooden spoon and scraping up any browned bits from bottom of pot.

3 Return meat to pot, along with any juices that have accumulated on plate. Pour in broth and stout and bring to a boil. Stir in carrots and potatoes and cover. Transfer pot to oven and bake until meat is fork-tender, potatoes are cooked through, and sauce has thickened slightly, about 1 hour. Season with salt and pepper. Serve hot.

ITALIAN STIR-FRY

with BEEF & SPRING VEGETABLES

WINE SUGGESTION: VALPOLICELLA

When most cooks think of stir-fries, they obviously think of Asian cooking. But the stir-fry technique can be applied to many ingredients and seasonings, as in this dish with Mediterranean flavors. This recipe also works well with thinly sliced pork tenderloin or chicken breast, both of which should be stir-fried for about 3 minutes in Step 3 to ensure they are thoroughly cooked.

YOU WILL NEED

1 pound boneless sirloin steak

2 tablespoons extra-virgin olive oil

1 yellow onion, halved lengthwise and cut into ¼-inch-thick half-moons

8 ounces asparagus, ends trimmed, cut into 1-inch lengths

1 small zucchini, trimmed, halved lengthwise, and cut into ¼-inch-thick half-moons

1 cup sugar snap peas, trimmed

1 garlic clove, minced

½ cup drained and chopped oil-packed sun-dried tomatoes

¼ cup coarsely chopped pitted Kalamata olives

2 teaspoons minced fresh oregano, or 1 teaspoon dried oregano

½ teaspoon kosher salt

⅛ teaspoon red pepper flakes

1 cup reduced-sodium chicken broth

1 tablespoon tomato paste

1 teaspoon cornstarch

Hot cooked small pasta, such as orzo or ditalini, for serving

1 If you have time, freeze steak for about 1 hour to firm for easier slicing. Trim off outside ring of fat on steak. Holding a large, sharp knife at a 45-degree angle, cut steak across grain into wide, thin slices.

2 Heat 1 tablespoon of oil in a very large sauté pan or wok over medium-high heat. Add onion, asparagus, zucchini, and sugar snaps. Stir-fry vegetables until crisp-tender, about 3 minutes. Add garlic and cook until fragrant, about 30 seconds. Stir in sun-dried tomatoes and olives and stir-fry until heated through, about 1 minute. Transfer vegetable mixture to a plate.

3 Heat remaining 1 tablespoon oil over medium-high heat. Add steak and season with oregano, salt, and red pepper flakes. Cook, stirring occasionally, just until it loses its pink color, about 1 $\frac{1}{2}$ minutes. Return vegetable mixture to skillet and stir-fry to mix well, about 1 minute.

4 In a small bowl, whisk together broth, tomato paste, and cornstarch until cornstarch dissolves. Add to beef mixture in sauté pan and stir just until liquid comes to a boil and thickens. Serve at once, spooned over pasta.

OVEN-POACHED
SALMON FILLETS
with WATERCRESS MAYONNAISE

MAIN COURSE

MAKES 4 SERVINGS

WINE SUGGESTION: UN-OAKED CALIFORNIA CHARDONNAY

Poaching fish in an herbed liquid adds both flavor and moisture, and oven-poaching is the easiest and most reliable version of this technique. Salmon's meaty texture holds up particularly well to poaching and is delectable served chilled. Here, it is paired with a watercress mayonnaise; its peppery spiciness and green color are perfect complements to the fish.

YOU WILL NEED

1 shallot, thinly sliced

4 sprigs fresh flat-leaf parsley, with stems

One 2-inch sprig fresh thyme. or $^1/_8$ teaspoon dried thyme

$^1/_3$ cup dry white wine, such as Pinot Grigio

$^1/_3$ cup water

Four 6-ounce salmon steaks

$^1/_4$ teaspoon salt

$^1/_8$ teaspoon freshly ground black pepper

WATERCRESS MAYONNAISE

$^1/_2$ cup packed watercress leaves

$^1/_3$ cup mayonnaise

1 tablespoon whole-grain Dijon mustard

2 teaspoons fresh lemon juice

1 Preheat oven to 350°F. Lightly oil a 9-by-13-inch stainless-steel, glass, or ceramic baking dish. (Do not use uncoated aluminum, as it could react with wine and give salmon a metallic flavor.)

2 Scatter shallot, parsley, and thyme over bottom of baking dish. Pour in wine and water. Place salmon on top of shallot mixture. Season with salt and pepper. Cover tightly with aluminum foil.

3 Bake until salmon is barely opaque outside and with a rosy center when prodded with tip of a knife, about 20 minutes. Uncover and let cool completely in dish. Cover tightly with plastic wrap and refrigerate until chilled (cooking juices will jell), at least 4 hours or overnight.

continued

④ To make watercress mayonnaise: Pulse watercress in a food processor to finely chop. Add mayonnaise, mustard, and lemon juice and process to combine. Transfer to a small serving bowl, cover, and refrigerate for at least 1 hour and up to 1 day.

⑤ Using a slotted spatula, transfer salmon steaks to a platter. Serve chilled, with sauce passed on side.

SCALLOPS & SNOW PEAS

with GINGER

Here is a recipe for a Chinese stir-fry that may keep you from ordering takeout. It does require an extra step, the authentic technique called velveting. A brief dip in simmering water gives the scallops a lush, velvety texture that you can't get from stir-frying alone. And remember, with stir-frying, once the chopping is done the dish cooks in minutes. A Chinese cook once taught us that if it takes longer to prepare and make the stir-fry than it does to cook the rice that goes with it, you are chopping too slowly.

YOU WILL NEED

SCALLOPS

2 tablespoons Chinese rice wine, sake, or dry sherry

3 quarter-sized slices peeled fresh ginger

1 ½ pounds sea scallops, rinsed, drained, patted dry, and halved horizontally

SEASONING MIXTURE NO. 1

2 tablespoons minced green onion, white part only

1 ½ tablespoons peeled and minced fresh ginger

3 garlic cloves, minced

¼ to ½ teaspoon red pepper flakes

SEASONING MIXTURE NO. 2

½ cup reduced-sodium chicken broth

3 ½ tablespoons soy sauce, preferably low-sodium

2 tablespoons Chinese rice wine, sake, or dry sherry

1 teaspoon sugar

1 tablespoon cornstarch

2 tablespoons vegetable oil

12 ounces snow peas, trimmed

1 large red bell pepper, seeded, deribbed, and cut into ½-inch squares

2 tablespoons thinly sliced green onion tops

2 teaspoons Asian sesame oil

Hot cooked rice, for serving

continued

1 To prepare scallops, stir rice wine and ginger slices together in a medium bowl, crushing ginger with spoon to release its flavor. Add scallops and toss gently. Cover with plastic wrap and refrigerate for 20 minutes.

2 To make seasoning mixtures, combine green onion, ginger, garlic, and pepper flakes in a small bowl. Combine broth, soy sauce, rice wine, and sugar in another bowl. Add cornstarch and stir to dissolve.

3 Bring a medium saucepan of water to a boil over high heat. Add scallops and their marinade and cook just until they turn opaque, about 30 seconds. Do not overcook. Drain and remove ginger.

4 Heat a wok or a large sauté pan over high heat. Add 1 tablespoon of vegetable oil and heat until shimmering. Add snow peas and bell pepper and cook, stirring and tossing, until vegetables are crisp-tender, 1 to 2 minutes. Transfer vegetable mixture to a bowl.

5 Return wok to high heat, add remaining 1 tablespoon oil and heat until very hot. Add green onion seasoning mixture and stir-fry until fragrant, about 10 seconds. Stir in broth seasoning mixture. Return scallops and vegetables to wok and stir until sauce boils and thickens and scallops are heated through, about 30 seconds. Transfer to a platter, sprinkle with green onion leaves, and drizzle with sesame oil. Serve hot, with rice.

FISH TACOS

with MANGO SALSA

BEER SUGGESTION: LAGER

Fish tacos have mainstreamed from their origins in San Diego taco stands. You can feel virtuous by choosing to make these instead of meat tacos with fried shells. Late spring is when mangoes are most abundant, and they make a sweet and spicy salsa. Most taco stands use two tortillas per taco to contain the juices, but at home you may get away with a single tortilla. Green cabbage will provide optimal taste in this recipe; however, you can also use very finely shredded purple cabbage for a festive look, as pictured.

YOU WILL NEED

FISH

1 tablespoon extra-virgin olive oil

1 tablespoon fresh lime juice

1 1/2 teaspoons chili powder

1/2 teaspoon kosher salt

1 1/4 pounds cod fillets or other firm-fleshed fish fillets

SALSA

3 ripe mangoes, pitted, peeled, and cut into 1/2-inch dice (see note, page 34)

2 tablespoons minced shallots or red onion

2 tablespoons minced fresh cilantro

2 tablespoons fresh lime juice

1 jalapeño chile, seeded and minced

Pinch of kosher salt

1 tablespoon extra-virgin olive oil

Twelve to twenty-four (6-inch) corn tortillas, heated according to package directions

1 cup finely shredded green or purple cabbage, for serving

1 To prepare fish: In a glass or ceramic baking dish, whisk together oil, lime juice, chili powder, and salt. Add cod and turn to coat with marinade. Cover with plastic wrap and refrigerate while making salsa.

2 To make salsa: Combine all salsa ingredients in a serving bowl. Cover and set aside at room temperature.

continued

3 Heat oil in a large nonstick skillet over medium heat. Add cod and cook, turning occasionally, until golden brown and opaque when pierced in thickest part with tip of a knife, 8 to 10 minutes. Transfer to a bowl and break fish into bite-sized chunks.

4 For each taco, fill a single tortilla (or two stacked tortillas) with some fish, a spoonful of salsa, and a sprinkle of cabbage. Fold in half and serve at once.

PEELING MANGOES: Place a fruit on its side on a work surface. The pit will be running horizontally through the center of the fruit. Using a sharp knife, cut off the top of the fruit just above the pit. Turn the mango flat side down and cut off the other side of the fruit. Using a large metal serving spoon, scoop the mango flesh from each portion in one piece. The peeled mango can now be sliced. Pare off the flesh remaining on the pit with a small knife to eat as your reward.

BRAISED RADISHES

with GREEN ONIONS

You've heard of thinking outside the box, but with radishes, we should think outside the salad bowl. When radishes are cooked, they lose some of their bite and acquire a mellow turnip taste. Make this in the spring with the freshest radishes (look for those with perky green tops), and you'll have a new favorite side dish. It's especially tasty with grilled fish fillets such as halibut.

YOU WILL NEED

2 bunches radishes, trimmed (about 20 radishes)

2 tablespoons unsalted butter

2 green onions, including green parts, chopped

Kosher salt and freshly ground black pepper

1 Place radishes in a large bowl of cold water and scrub to remove any grit. Drain. Using slicing disk on a food processor or a V-slicer, thinly slice radishes. (You should have 4 cups.)

2 Melt 1 tablespoon of butter in a large skillet over medium heat. Add green onions and cook until wilted, about 2 minutes. Add radishes and cook, stirring occasionally, until tender, about 8 minutes. Remove from heat and stir in remaining 1 tablespoon butter, which will create a light, creamy sauce. Season with salt and pepper. Transfer to a serving bowl and serve at once.

FETTUCCINE

PASTA

with ASPARAGUS & RICOTTA

MAKES 4—6 SERVINGS

WINE SUGGESTION: PINOT GRIGIO

This creamy pasta dish is perfect for a quick spring supper. Have the ricotta at room temperature, as cold ricotta would cool the pasta too much. Simply place the ricotta in a bowl on top of the stove as you prepare the rest of the ingredients, and it will warm up nicely.

YOU WILL NEED

1 1/2 pounds asparagus

1 pound fettuccine

1 1/2 cups ricotta cheese, at room temperature

1/2 cup (2 ounces) freshly grated Parmigiano-Reggiano, plus more for serving

3 tablespoons unsalted butter, at room temperature

3 tablespoons minced fresh chives and/or tarragon (preferably a combination)

Kosher salt and freshly ground black pepper

1. Bring a large pot of lightly salted water to a boil over high heat.

2. Snap off and discard woody ends of asparagus. Cut off spears about 1 inch below tips; reserve tips. Cut asparagus stalks into 1-inch lengths. Add stalks (not tips) to boiling water and cook for 1 1/2 minutes. Add tips and cook until asparagus is barely tender, about 3 minutes more. Using a large wire skimmer or a sieve, lift asparagus from water and transfer to a bowl. Do not rinse.

3. Add fettuccine to boiling water and cook according to package directions until al dente. During last minute of cooking, add asparagus to water to reheat it. Scoop out and reserve about 1/2 cup of cooking water, then drain fettuccine and asparagus and return them to pot.

4. Add ricotta, 1/2 cup Parmigiano-Reggiano, butter, and chives to pot and stir, adding enough of reserved cooking water to make a creamy sauce. Season generously with salt and pepper. Serve hot in individual bowls, with additional Parmigiano-Reggiano passed on side.

ASPARAGUS

with GREMOLATA BUTTER

Asparagus needs a gentle hand in seasoning, so use complementary flavors that enhance but don't overpower the delicious spears. Gremolata, a mix of lemon zest, parsley, and garlic, is usually served with the famous Italian dish of braised veal shanks, osso buco, but it can add spark to vegetables, too. The tips are more tender than the stalk, so to reduce the risk of overcooking, add the tips to the water after the stalks have cooked a bit.

YOU WILL NEED

2 pounds asparagus
2 tablespoons unsalted butter
1 garlic clove, minced
Finely grated zest of 1 lemon

1 tablespoon minced fresh flat-leaf parsley
2 tablespoons fresh lemon juice
Kosher salt

1 Snap off and discard woody ends of asparagus. Cut off spears about 1 inch below tips; reserve tips. Cut asparagus stalks into 1-inch lengths.

2 Bring a large sauté pan of lightly salted water to a boil over high heat. Add asparagus stalks (not tips) and cook for 1 ½ minutes. Add tips and cook until asparagus is barely tender, about 3 minutes more. Drain in a colander. Do not rinse under cold water. Wipe sauté pan dry.

3 In same pan, melt butter over medium-high heat. Add garlic and cook just until fragrant, about 30 seconds. Add asparagus, lemon zest, and parsley, stirring gently to coat asparagus. Remove from heat and stir in lemon juice. Season with salt. Transfer to a serving dish and serve hot.

ASPARAGUS

When the ground warms in spring, the shoots of the asparagus plant peek up through the soil. Before long, the shoots develop into thicker stalks that are harvested before they can grow into tall plants with feathery leaves.

The width of the asparagus stalk is directly related to its age, and the youngest asparagus is the thinnest. The woody stalk end should be snapped off where the stalk begins to become tender. Just bend each stalk to determine its breaking point. Some cooks like to peel asparagus, but it is really unnecessary, as commercial asparagus now has thin skin. If you do peel, use a swivel peeler on the lower part of the stalk only, and allow slightly less time for cooking. Asparagus is grown in sandy soil, so wash it well to remove any grit.

White asparagus, which is considered a delicacy in northern Europe and is becoming more popular here, too, is covered with dirt during growing, depriving it of sunlight and therefore of the chlorophyll that makes the stalks green. This technique gives the stalks a milder, refined flaver, too. White asparagus should be peeled before cooking. To store asparagus, keep the stalks moist by wrapping the cut ends in moist paper towels. Refrigerate in the vegetable crisper drawer for up to two days.

❧

STEAKHOUSE

CREAMED SPINACH

SIDE DISH

>>«<

MAKES 6 SERVINGS

Most Americans know creamed spinach as a staple at steakhouses, just the thing to set off a juicy grilled steak. This classic dish is always at its best when made with fresh spinach. It's worth the extra effort.

YOU WILL NEED

1 cup water

Kosher salt

Three 10-ounce bunches fresh spinach, well washed and stemmed

1 cup reduced-sodium chicken broth

$^{3}/_{4}$ cup heavy cream

3 tablespoons unsalted butter

1 garlic clove, minced

3 tablespoons all-purpose flour

A few gratings of nutmeg

Freshly ground black pepper

1 Bring water to a boil in a large saucepan over high heat and salt lightly. In batches, add spinach, stirring until each batch is wilted before adding next. Cover tightly, reduce heat to medium, and cook until spinach is tender, about 5 minutes.

2 Drain spinach in a colander over a large bowl. Measure 1 $^{1}/_{4}$ cups of cooking water and pour into a separate bowl. Add broth and cream and set aside.

3 Rinse spinach under cold water. A handful at a time, squeeze spinach to remove excess water. Coarsely chop spinach.

4 Heat butter and garlic in a medium skillet over medium-low heat just until butter melts. Whisk in flour and let bubble without browning for 2 minutes. Whisk in broth mixture and bring to a simmer. Cook, whisking often, until sauce is thickened and no raw flour taste remains, about 5 minutes. Stir in spinach and heat through, about 2 minutes. Season with nutmeg, salt, and pepper. Transfer to a serving bowl and serve hot.

KEY LIME CHEESECAKE

Cheesecake is a perennial favorite, and the sweet-yet-tart flavor of Key limes makes this one extraordinary. Serve the cheesecake as it is or top each slice with a tropical fruit salad of fresh papaya, mango, and banana.

YOU WILL NEED

CRUST

1 1/2 cups graham cracker crumbs (about 14 whole graham crackers)

6 tablespoons unsalted butter, melted

FILLING

Three 8-ounce packages cream cheese, at room temperature

1 cup granulated sugar

Freshly grated zest from 2 Key limes or 1 Persian lime

1 tablespoon cornstarch

3 large eggs, at room temperature

2/3 cup fresh lime juice, preferably from Key limes

1. Position racks in center and bottom third of oven and preheat oven to 300°F.

2. To make crust: Mix graham cracker crumbs and butter in a medium bowl until crumbs are evenly moistened. Press mixture onto bottom and partially up sides of a 9-inch springform pan. Refrigerate while making filling.

3. To make filling: Beat cream cheese, sugar, lime zest, and cornstarch in a large bowl with an electric mixer on high speed until smooth and fluffy, scraping down sides of bowl as needed. One at a time, beat in eggs, mixing just until blended and smooth. Reduce mixer speed to low and mix in lime juice. Do not overbeat or cheesecake will rise during baking, then sink and crack when cooled. Pour batter into prepared crust.

4. Place a baking pan half-filled with hot water on lower oven rack. Put cheesecake on center rack. Bake until edges are set and only very center of cheesecake appears slightly uncooked, 50 to 60 minutes. Turn off oven and prop door ajar with a wooden spoon. Let cheesecake cool in turned-off oven for at least 30 minutes. Transfer to a wire rack and let cool completely.

continued

5 Cover with plastic wrap and refrigerate until chilled, at least 4 hours or overnight. Just before serving, remove sides of pan. Using a sharp knife dipped into cold water, cut cheesecake into wedges and serve.

KEY LIMES

Key limes hail from the Florida Keys, where they have only recently become a commercial crop. Put a Key lime next to the common dark green Persian variety, and the distinction is obvious at a glance. The Key lime is much smaller, barely larger than a walnut. Its skin is pale green to yellow, and so thin that the zest must be removed with a Microplane zester. These limes, sold in mesh bags of about two dozen fruits, start showing up in the market in April, and their season runs through the summer.

The real difference is in the flavor, which is more tart than that of the Persian lime, yet at the same time more rounded. The next time you make a lime-based cocktail, such as a mojito or a margarita, try Key limes, and you are bound to experience a revelation. (Many of today's top mixologists insist on them for their cocktails.) And, as you would think, a Key lime pie made with the real McCoy is an eye-opener, too.

MANGO CASHEW CRISP

Mangoes, which taste like peaches on a tropical vacation, can be baked into cobblers, pies, and crisps. If ever there was a dessert for serving warm with vanilla ice cream, this is it. If you wish, add 3 tablespoons minced crystallized ginger to the mango filling.

YOU WILL NEED

TOPPING

1 cup old-fashioned (rolled) oatmeal

1/2 cup packed light brown sugar

1/2 cup all-purpose flour

1 cup (4 ounces) coarsely chopped cashews

1/2 cup (1 stick) unsalted butter, at room temperature

1 cup granulated sugar

1 tablespoon cornstarch

10 ripe mangoes, peeled, pitted, and cut into 1/2-inch-thick slices (see page 34)

Grated zest of 1 lime

2 tablespoons fresh lime juice

3 tablespoons cold unsalted butter, thinly sliced

1/2 gallon vanilla ice cream, for serving

1 Preheat oven to 350°F. Lightly butter a 9-by-13-inch baking dish.

2 To make topping: Using your fingers, mix oatmeal, brown sugar, and flour together in a medium bowl, being sure to break up any clumps of sugar. Mix in cashews. Add butter and work it in with your fingers until mixture is combined and crumbly.

3 Whisk sugar and cornstarch together in a large bowl. Add mangoes with lime zest and juice and toss gently to mix. Add butter. Pour into baking dish. Sprinkle topping evenly over fruit.

4 Bake until juices are bubbling and topping is crisp, about 40 minutes. If nuts threaten to burn, loosely cover crisp with aluminum foil. Cool for at least 10 minutes before serving warm or cooled to room temperature, with ice cream.

ALMOND MERINGUES

with STRAWBERRY COMPOTE

DESSERT

MAKES 8 SERVINGS

When you have great berries, as The Fresh Market does, you don't have to do much to set them off. These crisp meringues are great for a dinner party. Allow lots of time—three hours, to be precise—so they can dry completely. Or make them one day ahead, as they will benefit from an overnight stay in the turned-off oven. But don't try to make or store meringues during rainy or humid weather, as they will stay stubbornly sticky.

YOU WILL NEED

ALMOND MERINGUES

$1/2$ cup sliced almonds, toasted (see page 111)

$1/2$ cup confectioners' sugar

6 large egg whites, at room temperature

$1/8$ teaspoon cream of tartar

1 cup granulated sugar

$1/4$ teaspoon almond extract

STRAWBERRY COMPOTE

8 cups fresh strawberries, stemmed and thinly sliced

$1/4$ cup granulated sugar

1 tablespoon fresh lemon juice

WHIPPED CREAM

1 cup heavy cream

2 tablespoons confectioners' sugar

$1/2$ teaspoon vanilla extract

Mint sprigs, for garnish (optional)

1 Position racks in center and upper third of oven and preheat oven to 225°F. Line two baking sheets with parchment paper or silicone baking pads.

2 Process almonds and confectioners' sugar in a food processor until almonds are finely ground into a powder. Beat egg whites and cream of tartar in a large bowl with an electric mixer on low speed until whites are foamy. Increase speed to high and beat until whites form soft peaks. Still beating, add granulated sugar, 1 tablespoon at a time, and beat until whites are shiny and firm. Using a large rubber spatula, fold in ground almond mixture and almond extract just until incorporated.

continued

3 Using about ³/₄ cup for each meringue, drop mixture in mounds onto lined baking sheets, spacing them about 2 inches apart. Using back of a wet large spoon, spread each mound into a 4-inch-diameter round and make an indentation in center to form a shell.

4 Bake until meringues are crisp and pale beige, 2 ½ to 3 hours. Let cool for 10 minutes on baking sheet. (For extra-crisp meringues, turn off oven and let meringues stand in turned-off oven overnight.) Carefully peel meringues from paper. (Meringues can be stored in an airtight container at room temperature for up to 2 days.)

5 To make compote: Combine all compote ingredients in a large bowl. Cover and refrigerate for at least 1 or up to 8 hours.

6 To make whipped cream: Whip all ingredients together in a chilled medium bowl with an electric mixer on high speed until soft peaks form. Cover and refrigerate until ready to serve. (If cream separates, whisk it to recombine.)

7 To serve, place a meringue on each plate. Add a dollop of whipped cream and a spoonful of strawberry compote. Drizzle some strawberry juice over each filled meringue. Garnish with mint sprigs, if using, and serve at once.

VANILLA ICE CREAM *with*
· RHUBARB SAUCE ·

DESSERT

MAKES 6 SERVINGS

Rhubarb used to be known as "pie plant," because it was most often baked in a crust. There are many other uses for the red stalks (the leaves are toxic, so don't eat them), including this sauce for serving over ice cream or plain cake. Let the sauce cool for about 30 minutes before serving—you don't want it to melt the ice cream.

YOU WILL NEED

SAUCE

4 cups $1/4$-inch-sliced rhubarb (about 1 pound)

$3/4$ cup sugar, or more to taste

Freshly grated zest of $1/2$ large orange

$1 1/2$ teaspoons cornstarch

$1/2$ cup fresh orange juice

1 quart vanilla ice cream, for serving

1 To make sauce: Combine rhubarb, sugar, and orange zest in a medium nonreactive saucepan. Sprinkle cornstarch over orange juice in a small bowl and stir to dissolve cornstarch. Stir into rhubarb mixture. Bring to a simmer over medium heat, stirring often to help dissolve sugar. Cook at a brisk simmer, stirring occasionally, just until rhubarb is barely tender (it will soften more during cooling), 8 to 10 minutes.

2 Remove from heat and let cool until lukewarm, at least 30 minutes. Serve spooned over ice cream.

STRAWBERRY TART

DESSERT

MAKES 8 SERVINGS

with MASCARPONE FILLING

Good cooks have special recipes they can vary as needed to create reliably delicious dishes. That's how we feel about this almond pastry dough, which is also used for the Fresh Blueberry Tart on page 96. It can be pressed into a tart pan without being rolled out, and it makes a sweet dough that is like a crisp almond cookie. This filling couldn't be easier, and is the perfect showcase for the season's best strawberries.

YOU WILL NEED

ALMOND PASTRY DOUGH

¹/₃ cup sliced almonds

2 tablespoons sugar

1 cup unbleached all-purpose flour

¹/₄ teaspoon salt

¹/₂ cup (1 stick) cold unsalted butter, very thinly sliced

1 large egg yolk

¹/₄ teaspoon almond extract

FILLING

12 ounces mascarpone cheese, at room temperature

¹/₃ cup confectioners' sugar

1 teaspoon vanilla extract

Grated zest of 1 lemon

¹/₂ cup heavy cream

6 cups fresh strawberries, stemmed

¹/₂ cup strawberry preserves

2 tablespoons white rum or water

1 Preheat oven to 375°F. Lightly butter a 9-inch tart pan with a removable bottom.

2 To make dough: Pulse almonds and sugar together in a food processor until almonds are ground into a powder. Add flour and salt and pulse to combine. Add butter and pulse until mixture resembles coarse meal with some pea-sized pieces. Mix egg yolk with almond extract in a small bowl. With machine running, add yolk mixture through feed tube, then pulse just until dough begins to clump together. Do not overprocess. (Or, in batches, grind almonds and sugar in a blender. Transfer to a bowl and stir in flour. Using a pastry blender, cut in butter until mixture is crumbly, with some pea-sized pieces of butter. Stir in yolk and almond extract.)

continued

3 Gather dough and press evenly into pan with your fingers or a wooden tart tamper, being sure that sides and bottom meet at a sharp 90-degree angle (think of how a floor meets a wall). Pierce crust all over with a fork and cover pan with plastic wrap. Freeze until firm, 20 to 30 minutes.

4 Unwrap crust and line with lightly buttered aluminum foil, buttered side down. Fill pan with pastry weights or dried beans. Place on a baking sheet. Bake until crust looks set, about 12 minutes. Carefully remove foil and weights and continue baking until crust is golden brown, about 15 more minutes. Let cool completely on a wire rack.

5 To make filling: Using a rubber spatula, mix mascarpone, confectioners' sugar, vanilla, and lemon zest together in a medium bowl until blended. Whip cream in a chilled small bowl with an electric mixer on high speed until it forms soft peaks. Fold into mascarpone mixture. Spread filling in cooled tart shell.

6 Arrange berries, stemmed side down, in concentric circles on top of filling. Bring preserves and rum to a boil in a small saucepan over medium heat. Simmer for 2 minutes. Strain through a sieve into a small bowl and let cool slightly. Brush warm strawberry glaze over strawberries. Refrigerate for up to 4 hours. Remove sides of tart pan. Cut tart into wedges and serve chilled.

STRAWBERRIES

Spring is the traditional season for red, juicy strawberries.
In fact, the most common type is actually called June-bearing,
which produces a single flush of flowers yielding one harvest.
The two other types, day-neutral and everbearing, have much longer
seasons. In most cases, when your local season arrives, you only have
a three- or four-week window of opportunity to buy them.
Mass production in warm-weather states has made strawberries
a year-round crop; however, even in California, spring is
the main harvest time.

Perhaps the most important point to remember about
strawberries is that they do not ripen after they are picked, so buy
evenly deep red berries without any pale green "shoulders." Store
them in the refrigerator, and do not wash or stem them until just
before eating. An unimportant, but interesting, factoid:
Strawberries are the only fruit with the seeds on the outside.

MENU
BUILDER

BEVERAGES & APPETIZER

GF ☙ Blueberry Chutney over Brie 55

DF GF ☙ Summer Fruit Sangría 57

DF GF ☙ Melon Agua Fresca 58

SOUPS & SALADS

☙ Summer Minestrone 59

GF ☙ Cold Corn Bisque with Pesto Swirl 60

DF GF ☙ Heirloom Tomato & Corn Salad 63

DF GF Italian Shrimp & Rice Salad 64

GF ☙ Two-Bean Salad with Cherry Tomatoes 66

MAIN COURSES

DF GF Marinated Chicken with Basil Drizzle 67

Pork Chops with Champagne Grape Sauce 72

DF Hamburgers with Roast-Pepper Ketchup 73

DF Carolina-Style Pulled Pork 74

Baby Back Ribs with Grilled Peaches 77

DF GF Cedar-Planked Salmon with Cucumber Salsa 79

DF Grilled Rib-Eye Steak with Coffeehouse Rub 83

☙ Rice Tian with Chard & Zucchini 84

GF ☙ Zucchini Pie with Polenta Crust 86

☙ Grilled Eggplant & Fontina Sandwiches 87

☙ Grill-Baked Ratatouille Casserole 88

☙ Grilled White Pizza with Zucchini 91

PASTAS

☙ Grilled Pasta Sauce with Tomatoes & Basil 93

Farfalle with Arugula & Sausage 94

DESSERTS

GF ☙ Ice Cream Sundaes with Grilled Pineapple & Caramel-Rum Sauce 95

☙ Fresh Blueberry Tart 96

☙ Bing Cherry Galette 99

☙ Peach-Pecan Shortcake 101

DF GF ☙ Melon & Lime Ice Pops 105

DF ‖ DAIRY-FREE   GF ‖ GLUTEN-FREE   ☙ ‖ VEGAN   ❦ ‖ VEGETARIAN

SUMMER

SUMMER BRINGS US A BOUNTY

OF FRUITS AND VEGETABLES, EVEN TO
THE POINT WHERE YOU MAY FIND
YOUR KITCHEN BURSTING WITH
EXCESS PRODUCE.

*The sweetness of corn, the pleasing tart juice
of tomatoes, the spice of basil—these flavors
never taste better than when they are enjoyed
in the summer sun. The same can be said of
summer fruits, such as melons, berries, and
stone fruits, whose traditional seasons never
seem long enough. Now, the grill is put to good
use at backyard cookouts featuring ribs, grilled
chicken, and more.*

BLUEBERRY CHUTNEY

APPETIZER

MAKES 4—6 SERVINGS

over BRIE

WINE SUGGESTION: SPANISH *or* FRENCH ROSÉ

This tasty appetizer, which balances the sweet flavor of blueberries with buttery Brie, will be ready in minutes, and it is likely to disappear from the table in record time, too. It works especially well with Brie, but try it over goat cheese or even a sharp Cheddar.

YOU WILL NEED

2 tablespoons sliced almonds

1 teaspoon vegetable oil

1 tablespoon minced shallot

1 small garlic clove, minced

$1/4$ cup honey

2 teaspoons balsamic vinegar

$1/2$ teaspoon minced fresh rosemary, plus more for garnish

$1/2$ teaspoon dry mustard

$1/8$ teaspoon red pepper flakes

One 6-ounce container fresh blueberries (about 1 $1/3$ cups)

1 small wheel ripe Brie (12 to 14 ounces), top rind trimmed off, at room temperature

Crackers, for serving

1 Heat a medium skillet over medium heat. Add almonds and cook, stirring constantly, until toasted, about 2 minutes. Transfer to a plate.

2 Add oil to skillet and heat over medium heat. Add shallot and garlic and cook, stirring occasionally, until tender, about 2 minutes. Add honey, balsamic vinegar, $1/2$ teaspoon rosemary, mustard, and pepper flakes and bring to a simmer, stirring to dissolve mustard. Add blueberries and cook just until warmed through without bursting, about 1 minute.

3 Place cheese on a serving platter. Pour blueberry chutney on top and garnish with toasted almonds and additional rosemary. Serve at once, with crackers.

SUMMER FRUIT SANGRÍA

BEVERAGE

DF | GF | Y | U

MAKES 6 SERVINGS

Sangría is a quintessential hot-weather quencher that should come with a warning label on each glass—it goes down easily, but it packs a punch. You can add or substitute other fruits, such as apricots or nectarines for the peaches, and raspberries or blackberries for the strawberries, as you wish.

YOU WILL NEED

2 ripe peaches, peeled, pitted, and cut into $1/2$-inch cubes

1 cup stemmed and sliced fresh strawberries

$1/2$ cup brandy

$1/4$ cup sugar

One 750-ml bottle fruity red wine such as Merlot

1 Combine peaches, strawberries, brandy, and sugar in a medium bowl. Cover and refrigerate, stirring often, until sugar dissolves, about 1 hour.

2 Mix wine with fruit and its liquid in a large pitcher. Cover and refrigerate until well chilled, at least 2 hours or up to 8 hours. Serve chilled.

MELON AGUA FRESCA

BEVERAGE

MAKES 6 SERVINGS

Agua fresca, the Mexican drink of fresh fruit puréed with water, tastes like summer in a glass. It is refreshing at any time of day—try it instead of orange juice for breakfast—but it can also be the base for a cocktail, spiked with tequila or golden rum. The formula for agua fresca is always the same: 8 cups of fruit puréed with sugar and lime juice to taste, diluted with 12 ounces of chilled club soda or water. The fruit choices are almost endless. Adjust the taste as needed with a bit more sugar or lime juice.

YOU WILL NEED

8 cups 1-inch chunks ripe cantaloupe (1 large cantaloupe)

2 tablespoons sugar, or as needed

2 tablespoons fresh lime juice, or as needed

1 ½ cups chilled club soda or water

Mint sprigs, for garnish (optional)

1. Purée melon in a food processor or blender. Add 2 tablespoons sugar and 2 tablespoons lime juice and process to dissolve sugar. Taste and add more sugar or lime juice as needed. Transfer to a large pitcher. Cover and refrigerate until well chilled, at least 2 hours or overnight.

2. Just before serving, stir in club soda. Serve chilled, and garnish each serving with a mint sprig, if using.

HONEYDEW AGUA FRESCA: Substitute 8 cups ripe honeydew melon chunks (1 small honeydew melon) for cantaloupe.

MANGO OR PEACH AGUA FRESCA: Substitute 8 cups ripe mango chunks or peach slices (about 8 mangoes or 10 peaches) for cantaloupe.

STRAWBERRY AGUA FRESCA: Substitute 8 cups stemmed and sliced strawberries for cantaloupe.

SUMMER MINESTRONE

SOUP

MAKES 8 SERVINGS

WINE SUGGESTION: PINOT GRIGIO

There are two kinds of minestrone (which means "big soup" in Italian). In winter months, the soup is made with meat, sprinkled with cheese, and served piping hot. But in summer, this lighter version is delicious and satisfying, ladled into bowls and served at room temperature, a difference that makes lots of sense.

YOU WILL NEED

$^1/_4$ cup extra-virgin olive oil, plus more for drizzling

1 large yellow onion, chopped

2 carrots, peeled and cut into $^1/_2$-inch dice

2 celery stalks with leaves, cut into $^1/_2$-inch dice

4 garlic cloves, minced

1 teaspoon fennel seeds

2 teaspoons minced fresh sage

$^1/_2$ teaspoon red pepper flakes

3 cups canned reduced-sodium chicken or vegetable broth

One 28-ounce can white (cannellini) beans, rinsed and drained

1 large zucchini, trimmed and cut into $^1/_4$-inch thick rounds

6 ripe plum (Roma) tomatoes, seeded and diced

1 head escarole (9 ounces), well washed and coarsely chopped

Kosher salt

8 slices crusty Italian bread such as ciabatta, toasted

Freshly grated Parmigiano-Reggiano, for serving

1 In a large soup pot, heat $^1/_4$ cup oil over medium heat. Add onion, carrots, celery, and garlic. Cover and cook, stirring often, until vegetables are softened, about 10 minutes.

2 Stir in fennel, sage, and pepper flakes. Add broth, beans, zucchini, tomatoes, and enough water to cover beans by $^1/_2$ inch. Bring to a boil. A handful at a time, stir in escarole, letting each batch wilt before adding another. Reduce heat to medium-low and simmer, uncovered, until soup is well flavored, about 30 minutes. Season with salt. Let cool to room temperature.

3 To serve, place a slice of bread in each of 8 soup bowls and ladle in soup. Drizzle each with some olive oil and a sprinkling of Parmigiano-Reggiano, and serve.

COLD CORN BISQUE

with PESTO SWIRL

SOUP

MAKES 6—8 SERVINGS

WINE SUGGESTION: CALIFORNIA SAUVIGNON BLANC

This light and versatile soup is rich with the taste of corn—even the cobs are simmered to extract every bit of flavor. Many corn soups are of the rib-sticking chowder variety, made with potatoes and bacon, and too heavy for summer dining. This one is made with olive oil, because butter will harden when chilled and give the cold soup a gritty texture. Substitute a vegetable broth for the chicken broth to make excellent vegetarian soup as well as a gluten-free dish.

YOU WILL NEED

Kernels cut from 6 ears of corn, cobs reserved (see note)

6 cups reduced-sodium chicken or vegetable broth

2 tablespoons extra-virgin olive oil

2 celery stalks, chopped

1 cup chopped green onions, including green parts (about 4 green onions)

2 teaspoons cornstarch

1/2 cup half-and-half or heavy cream

Kosher salt and freshly ground black pepper

1/2 cup Pesto (page 171), at room temperature, for serving

1 Cut reserved cobs into large chunks. Bring cobs and broth to a boil in a large pot over high heat. Reduce heat to low and cover, leaving lid askew. Simmer for 45 minutes. Strain corn broth into a heatproof bowl and set aside (discard cobs).

2 In same pot, heat oil over medium heat. Add celery and cover. Cook, stirring often, until celery is tender, about 5 minutes. Add green onions and cook, uncovered, until wilted and fragrant, about 3 minutes. Add corn broth and corn kernels and bring to a simmer. Cook, uncovered, until kernels are tender, about 5 minutes.

3 In a small bowl, sprinkle cornstarch over half-and-half and whisk to dissolve. Stir into soup and bring to a boil to lightly thicken soup. Season with salt and pepper. In batches, purée soup in a blender with lid ajar and pour into a large bowl. Let cool to room temperature. Cover with plastic wrap and refrigerate until chilled, at least 4 hours or up to 1 day.

4 Just before serving, reseason soup with salt and pepper. Ladle soup into bowls and top each with about 1 tablespoon pesto. Using tip of spoon, swirl pesto into soup. Serve chilled.

CUTTING CORN KERNELS: Using a large knife, trim the pointed end from an ear of corn and stand it on end. Cut off the kernels by cutting down the cob where the kernels meet the cob. Transfer the kernels to a bowl. Working over a bowl, scrape the cob to extract the milk, if desired.

CORN

Corn on the cob is an appropriate dish for a Fourth of July cookout, because it is native to the Americas. Other vegetables with this pedigree include squash, beans, tomatoes, and blueberries, which are also likely to show up at a summer picnic.

Corn is always best when it comes from a local source. After corn is picked, its natural sugars convert fairly quickly to starch, so the freshest corn will also be the sweetest. Choose ears of corn with brightly colored moist husks and tassels. Pull the husk back a little to reveal the kernels—they should look plump and run to the top of the cob. Cook fresh corn as soon as possible, though it can be stored in a plastic bag in the refrigerator for up to 24 hours.

≫❦≪

TOMATO & CORN SALAD

SALAD

MAKES 6—8 SERVINGS

You won't have a wide window of opportunity to make this salad—only a few weeks in summer when both corn and tomatoes are at their peak. The corn must be sweet and fresh and the tomatoes must be juicy and flavorful. Use an assortment of heirloom tomatoes, which are available in many shapes, sizes, and colors.

YOU WILL NEED

4 ripe large heirloom tomatoes, or an assortment of large and small tomatoes

Kosher salt

2 tablespoons balsamic vinegar

$^1/_2$ cup extra-virgin olive oil

2 cups fresh corn kernels (4 to 5 ears of corn); see page 61

$^1/_4$ cup chopped fresh basil

Freshly ground black pepper

1 Using a serrated knife, cut each tomato in half lengthwise. Using your finger, poke out and discard seeds. Cut tomatoes into $^3/_4$-inch cubes. Toss tomatoes with $^1/_2$ teaspoon salt in a medium bowl. Let stand for 20 minutes. (This step extracts excess juices from tomatoes so they don't dilute vinaigrette.) Drain tomatoes.

2 Pour balsamic vinegar into a large bowl. Gradually whisk in oil. Add tomatoes, corn, and basil and toss. Season with salt and pepper. Serve at once, or cover and let stand for up to 2 hours at room temperature.

SHRIMP & RICE SALAD

Shrimp and rice salad, a colorful and tasty summer dish, is popular in Italy, where it is a staple on restaurant antipasti tables. When making your own, remember one important caveat: Never serve ice-cold rice salad. Starches in rice harden when chilled, so remove the salad from the refrigerator (or cooler) at least 30 minutes before serving so the rice can soften to its natural texture, then add the chilled shrimp. If you wish, add a cup or two of freshly cooked or thawed frozen peas to the salad with the shrimp and basil.

YOU WILL NEED

1 1/2 pounds large (21 to 25 count) shrimp, preferably wild-caught

2 cups Arborio rice

2 cups cherry or grape tomatoes, halved lengthwise

3 tablespoons white or red wine vinegar

1/2 teaspoon kosher salt

1/8 teaspoon red pepper flakes

2/3 cup extra-virgin olive oil

3 tablespoons chopped fresh basil, plus more for garnish

1 Bring a large saucepan of lightly salted water to a boil over high heat. Add shrimp and cook until they turn opaque, about 3 minutes. Rinse under cold running water and drain. Peel and devein shrimp. Transfer to a bowl, cover, and refrigerate until chilled, at least 1 hour or up to 1 day.

2 Bring a large saucepan of lightly salted water to a boil over high heat. Add rice and cook, uncovered, until tender, about 20 minutes. Drain in a fine-mesh sieve and rinse under cold water; drain again. Transfer to a large bowl and add cherry tomatoes.

3 In a small bowl, whisk vinegar, salt, and pepper flakes together. Gradually whisk in oil. Pour about two-thirds of dressing over rice and mix. Separately cover and refrigerate salad and remaining dressing for at least 2 hours or up to 8 hours.

4 At least 30 minutes or up to 1 hour before serving, remove rice salad from the refrigerator and let stand at room temperature. Add enough reserved dressing to moisten salad. Stir in shrimp and 3 tablespoons basil. Garnish with more chopped basil and serve immediately.

OUR SHRIMP

From the day we opened our doors, The Fresh Market has provided our customers with the safest, most delicious seafood available anywhere. You will always find wild American shrimp for sale in our fish department. With a nutritious diet determined entirely by nature, these shrimp have a unique flavor profile that is simply not found in other shrimp. Customers in each of our southern coast areas are offered shrimp from their own state, while stores in other states can buy shrimp caught off the coast of North or South Carolina.

One of the greatest challenges facing the seafood industry is the limited availability of wild seafood in a world with growing demand. In order for seafood to remain an affordable part of a healthy diet, the industry must continue to develop a responsible approach to sustainable aquaculture, including farm-raised shrimp.

>)<

TWO-BEAN SALAD

with CHERRY TOMATOES

Three-bean salad is a summer barbecue staple. Try this two-bean variation made with bright cherry tomatoes completing the trio, topped with shallot dressing.

YOU WILL NEED

VINAIGRETTE

¼ cup red wine vinegar

3 tablespoons minced shallots

2 teaspoons minced fresh thyme, or ¾ teaspoon dried thyme

½ teaspoon kosher salt

¼ teaspoon freshly ground black pepper

¾ cup extra-virgin olive oil

12 ounces green beans, trimmed and cut into 1 ½-inch lengths

One 15-ounce can pink beans, rinsed and drained

2 cups cherry or grape tomatoes, halved lengthwise

Kosher salt and freshly ground black pepper

4 ounces fresh white goat cheese, crumbled (optional)

1 To make vinaigrette, whisk vinegar, shallots, thyme, salt, and pepper together in a medium bowl. Gradually whisk in oil. Cover and set aside.

2 Bring a large pot of lightly salted water to a boil over high heat. Add green beans and cook, uncovered, until beans are bright green and crisp-tender, 3 to 5 minutes. Do not overcook. Using a wire skimmer or sieve, transfer beans to a large bowl of iced water. Let stand for 2 minutes to stop cooking. Drain well. Pat beans dry with paper towels.

3 No more than 30 minutes before serving, toss green beans, pink beans, tomatoes, and vinaigrette in a large bowl and season with salt and pepper. Top with crumbled cheese, if using, and serve immediately.

MARINATED CHICKEN

with BASIL DRIZZLE

MAIN COURSE

DF | GF | 🍷

MAKES 4 SERVINGS

WINE SUGGESTION: DOLCE ROSSO

Summer is the time for aromatic fresh basil. It can be a challenge not to put it into everything you cook (and we admit, we use it a lot in the recipes in this chapter). Here it becomes a quick and easy sauce for grilled chicken. Grilling the chicken over medium heat ensures that it cooks through without the flare-ups that can drive the grill cook crazy.

YOU WILL NEED

MARINADE

1 cup dry white wine, such as Pinot Grigio

Grated zest of 1 lemon

2 tablespoons fresh lemon juice

2 garlic cloves, minced

1 teaspoon kosher salt

1/2 teaspoon freshly ground black pepper

1/4 cup extra-virgin olive oil

Four 8-ounce boneless, skinless chicken breast halves

BASIL DRIZZLE

1 garlic clove, crushed and peeled

1/2 cup packed fresh basil leaves

2 tablespoons coarsely chopped fresh flat-leaf parsley

1 tablespoon balsamic vinegar

1/3 cup extra-virgin olive oil

Kosher salt and freshly ground black pepper

1 To make marinade: Whisk wine, lemon zest and juice, garlic, salt, and pepper together in a medium bowl. Gradually whisk in oil.

2 Place a chicken breast half between sheets of plastic wrap. Using the flat side of a meat pounder, pound the chicken until it has an even thickness of about 1/2 inch. Repeat with the remaining chicken breasts.

3 Pour marinade into a large self-sealing plastic bag. Add chicken and turn to coat. Press air out of bag and close bag. Refrigerate, turning the chicken occasionally, for at least 1 or up to 3 hours, no longer.

continued

4 Prepare an outdoor grill for direct cooking over medium (400°F) heat.

5 Meanwhile, make drizzle: With machine running, drop garlic through feed tube of a food processor or blender to mince. Add basil, parsley, and vinegar and pulse until minced. With machine running, gradually add oil to emulsify, stopping to scrape down sides of container as needed, and process until smooth. Season with salt and pepper. Set aside.

6 Brush grill grate clean. Remove chicken from marinade and shake off the excess marinade. Place on grill and close grill lid. Cook until lightly browned on bottom, about 6 minutes. Turn and cook until other side is browned and chicken feels firm when pressed in thickest part with a finger, about 6 minutes more. If flare-ups occur (though they shouldn't if lid is closed), move chicken to a cooler part of the grill, such as edges of grill grate of a charcoal grill or a turned-off burner of a gas grill. Remove chicken from grill, tent with aluminum foil, and let stand for 5 minutes.

7 Transfer each chicken breast half to a dinner plate and drizzle with about 1 tablespoon of basil drizzle; serve at once.

OUR CHICKEN

The Fresh Market is proud to offer all-natural chickens, whole and in a wide array of cuts for all your cooking needs. These birds have never been given antibiotics—a common procedure with factory-farmed poultry. Our chickens are raised in a spacious environment, which produces more tender meat. And they are fed a 100-percent vegetarian diet, without any animal by-products.

>)-((

GRILLING 101

Too often, cooks just throw food on the grill and hope for the best. With only a few essential techniques, you can be a grill master.

CHARCOAL VS. GAS: There is quite a debate raging about which kind of grill is better. It is not really a question of quality, but convenience. Charcoal does add an inimitable smoky taste to grilled meats. But on a weeknight, it's easier to turn on the gas grill. The choice is yours. Serious grillers have both kinds!

DIRECT AND INDIRECT HEAT: How the food is positioned over the heat source affects the cooking:

Direct cooking is cooking food directly over hot coals or the burners of a gas grill. This is reserved for foods that will cook in about 20 minutes, such as burgers, steaks, boneless chicken, and frankfurters. For a charcoal grill, you will need an empty area where you can move food that is cooking too quickly or dripping fat and causing flare-ups. Leave a perimeter around the mound of coals for this purpose. If flare-ups occur with a gas grill, move the food to a turned-off burner.

Indirect cooking refers to placing food away from the heat source so it cooks by radiated heat, though some foods may be seared over direct heat first before being moved to the cool side of the grill to cook by indirect heat. This method is reserved for large cuts of meat—roasts, bone-in or whole chicken, and ribs. For a charcoal grill, heap the coals on one side of the grill. For a gas grill, preheat the grill on high, then turn one burner off. For both, place a disposable aluminum foil pan on the empty side of the fuel bed. Pour about 2 cups of water into the pan and cook the food over the drip pan.

Barbecuing is cooking with indirect heat while adding smoke provided by wood chunks or chips that have been soaked in cold water for at least 30 minutes. Wood chunks work best when added to lit charcoal (wood chips can be used, too). For a gas grill, use wood chips placed in the metal smoker box recommended by the brand. Here's a useful tip: Start with dry chips in the box, let them ignite, then add drained wood chips.

USING LUMP CHARCOAL: The Fresh Market sells natural lump charcoal without additives. It burns at a higher temperature than briquettes and doesn't have the additives in briquettes that cause off odors. A charcoal chimney with newspaper crumpled in the bottom is the best way to start the first coals—lighting fluid is totally unnecessary and also adds off flavors to the food. Mound more charcoal over the lighted coals and let the coals burn until they are covered with white ash. Spread the charcoal in the grill, but leave a 4-inch perimeter around coals for direct heat so you have someplace to move the food when it drips its fat; for indirect heat, the coals should be on one side of the grill. Charcoal burns hottest during the first 20 minutes, then drops heat fairly rapidly. If you are cooking with indirect heat, you will have to add a few lumps every half hour or so to the coals to keep the temperature consistent.

KNOW YOUR HEAT: In general, for grilling, high heat is 450°F to 600°F, medium heat runs 350° to 450°F, and low heat is 275° to 350°F. It is easy to adjust the heat on gas grills, as most of them have thermometers in their lids that can be regulated with a twist of a knob. You can also place an oven thermometer in the grill. The heat in a charcoal grill can be changed by the amount of coals used (lots of charcoal for high heat and less for lower temperatures). To check an accurate reading in a charcoal grill, drop a candy thermometer (with a round glass face and a metal stem) through the top vent of the lid.

KEEP THE LID ON: Fire needs oxygen to stay alive, so a closed lid reduces the chances of flare-ups, most of which are caused by the marinade or fat dripping from the food onto the heat source. If you have a charcoal grill, the vents on the lid and underneath the kettle can be opened or shut to control the air flow. For high heat, keep the vents wide open to feed the flame. For medium heat, close them halfway to reduce the oxygen so the fire burns at a lower temperature. Close the vents only when you want to cut off the oxygen completely to shut the grill down.

PORK CHOPS

with CHAMPAGNE GRAPE SAUCE

MAIN COURSE

MAKES 4 SERVINGS

WINE SUGGESTION: OREGON PINOT NOIR

Fruit partners well with pork, as in this easy dish with a sauce that incorporates tiny purple champagne grapes. These little nuggets of sweetness can be used in cooking if they are barely warmed through and not allowed to burst. Their name is deceptive, because they are not the grapes fermented into Champagne; "champagne grapes" is the U.S. marketing name for fresh Black Corinth grapes, which become Zante currants when dried.

YOU WILL NEED

4 boneless pork chops, cut about 1 inch thick

Kosher salt and freshly ground black pepper

$^1/_4$ cup all-purpose flour

1 tablespoon vegetable oil

2 tablespoons unsalted butter

2 tablespoons minced shallots

$^2/_3$ cup dry white wine such as Pinot Grigio

$^2/_3$ cup reduced-sodium chicken broth

$^2/_3$ cup heavy cream

1 cup stemmed champagne grapes

1 teaspoon minced fresh tarragon

1 Season pork chops with 1 teaspoon salt and $^1/_2$ teaspoon pepper. Dredge in flour and shake off excess. In a large skillet, heat oil over medium heat. Add pork chops and cook until lightly browned, about 3 minutes on each side. Transfer to a plate.

2 Add butter and shallots to skillet and cook, stirring often, over medium heat until shallots are tender, about 2 minutes. Add wine and bring to a boil over high heat, scraping up any browned bits in skillet with a wooden spoon. Stir in broth and cream and boil over high heat until reduced by half, about 5 minutes. Return chops and any juices on plate to skillet and reduce heat to medium. Cook, occasionally turning chops in sauce, until sauce is thick enough to coat a spoon and chops are barely pink in center when pierced with tip of a sharp knife, 2 to 3 minutes. Transfer chops to a platter.

3 Add grapes and tarragon to sauce and cook just until grapes are warm, about 30 seconds. Season with salt and pepper. Pour sauce over chops and serve.

HAMBURGERS

with ROAST-PEPPER KETCHUP

WINE SUGGESTION: SPANISH RIOJA

For the juiciest burgers, use ground chuck. Ground sirloin is lean and flavorful, but can make burgers that are a bit firm. Another tip: Add salt and pepper to the meat before forming the patties so the seasoning can be savored in every bite. As for the ketchup, you will be surprised at how this simple combination can add a touch of class to the humble burger.

ROAST-PEPPER KETCHUP
One 12-ounce jar roasted red peppers, rinsed and drained

³/₄ cup ketchup

1 ¹/₃ pounds ground chuck
1 ¹/₄ teaspoons kosher salt

¹/₂ teaspoon freshly ground black pepper

4 hamburger buns

Mustard, mayonnaise, sliced onion, lettuce leaves, and sliced tomatoes, for serving

1 To make ketchup: Purée peppers in a food processor or blender. Add ketchup and process until combined. Transfer to a bowl, cover, and set aside at room temperature for up to 2 hours.

2 Prepare an outdoor grill for direct cooking over high (500°F) heat.

3 Mix ground chuck, salt, and pepper together with your hands in a medium bowl. Do not over-handle meat. Lightly form into 4 patties about 1 inch thick.

4 Brush grill grate clean. Add burgers and close grill lid. Cook until burgers are browned on bottom, about 3 minutes. Flip burgers over and continue cooking with lid closed until other side is browned and a burger feels only slightly resilient when pressed in center with a fingertip, 3 to 4 minutes more for medium-rare.

5 Meanwhile, open buns and toast on edges of grill grate until warm and lightly browned. Place cooked burgers in buns and pass ketchup on side. Let everyone pick their own fixings from mustard, mayonnaise, onion, lettuce, and tomatoes.

PULLED PORK

WINE SUGGESTION: ZINFANDEL

The Fresh Market headquarters are in North Carolina, so we have eaten our share of the famous local barbecue. Every region of this country has a tradition of outdoor cooking with locally harvested fuel (even a clambake is a kind of barbecue). Carolina barbecue is traditionally cooked over hickory wood and served with a thin vinegar-based sauce. So, get up early one weekend morning, put on a big pork shoulder, and invite a bunch of friends over for barbecue in the afternoon.

YOU WILL NEED

SAUCE

1 cup distilled white vinegar

$^{1}/_{4}$ cup sugar

2 tablespoons ketchup

1 teaspoon cayenne pepper

2 garlic cloves, minced

$^{1}/_{2}$ teaspoon kosher salt

RUB

1 tablespoon kosher salt

1 tablespoon Hungarian sweet paprika

2 teaspoons granulated garlic

2 teaspoons granulated onion

1 teaspoon freshly ground black pepper

$^{1}/_{2}$ teaspoon cayenne pepper

PORK

One 7 $^{1}/_{2}$-pound boneless pork shoulder, tied

2 handfuls hickory wood chips, soaked in water for 30 minutes (plus 1 handful dry wood chips, if using a gas grill)

12 soft sandwich rolls, for serving

1 To make sauce: Whisk all sauce ingredients together in a small bowl to dissolve sugar. (Or shake ingredients in a jar.) Let stand at room temperature while cooking pork.

2 To make rub: Mix all rub ingredients together in a small bowl. Generously season pork all over with spice mixture and rub it in. Cover loosely with plastic wrap and let stand at room temperature for 1 hour. (Pork can be rubbed day before, wrapped tightly in plastic wrap and refrigerated. Remove pork from refrigerator 1 hour before cooking).

3 Prepare an outdoor grill for indirect cooking with very low (300°F) heat. If using a gas grill with a smoker box, add dry chips to box and let them ignite.

4 Scatter a handful of drained wood chips over coals in a charcoal grill or add to a smoker box for a gas grill according to manufacturer's instructions. Place pork on grill over pan and close grill lid. Cook with lid closed as much as possible (adding remaining drained wood chips to grill after 45 minutes) for 3 hours. Turn pork over and grill with lid closed until pork is fork-tender, very dark brown, and an instant-read thermometer inserted in center of pork registers 185°F, about 3 hours more. (Be flexible with your time and err on long side, if you have to.) Remove pork from grill. Double-wrap pork in aluminum foil and let stand for 30 minutes. (This allows pork to continue cooking with residual heat so that it is even more tender.)

5 To serve, unwrap pork on a carving board. Using two forks, pull apart and shred meat. Or, cut meat across grain into $^{1}/_{2}$-inch-thick slices and coarsely chop with a large knife. Transfer meat to a bowl. Serve meat on rolls, with sauce passed on side.

BABY BACK RIBS

with GRILLED PEACHES

MAIN COURSE

MAKES 6 SERVINGS

WINE SUGGESTION: MERLOT

Authentic long-cooked barbecue is great, but what do you do when you are short on time yet want succulent ribs with a spicy rub and sweet glaze? Use this reliable method, where the ribs are wrapped in foil to simmer in their own juices on the grill, then browned and glazed over direct heat. Grilled peaches add summer color and flavor to the platter.

YOU WILL NEED

Three 2 $^3/_4$-pound racks baby back ribs

RUB

2 tablespoons chili powder

1 tablespoon plus 2 teaspoons kosher salt

1 $^1/_2$ teaspoons freshly ground black pepper

1 teaspoon granulated garlic

1 teaspoon granulated onion

$^1/_2$ teaspoon cayenne pepper

GLAZE

$^3/_4$ cup peach preserves

2 tablespoons unsalted butter

2 tablespoons ketchup

2 tablespoons cider vinegar

2 tablespoons bourbon or water

2 teaspoons hickory liquid smoke

PEACHES

3 ripe peaches, halved and pitted

1 tablespoon unsalted butter, melted

Freshly ground black pepper

1 To prepare ribs: On bone side of ribs, at corner of rack, slip a small knife under membrane. Grab membrane with a paper towel and pull it off. (You may have to make a few attempts.) Cut each rack in half to make 6 slabs total.

2 To make rub: Mix all rub ingredients together in a small bowl. Season ribs all over with rub. Double-wrap each slab in heavy-duty aluminum foil. Let stand at room temperature for 15 to 30 minutes.

3 Prepare an outdoor grill for direct cooking over medium (425°F) heat.

continued

4 Place ribs on grill grate and close grill lid. Grill, turning occasionally with tongs, being careful not to tear foil, until ribs are tender (carefully open a foil packet to check), about 45 minutes. Remove from grill. Let cool slightly, then unwrap and discard juices. (Ribs can be prepared to this point about 1 hour ahead, or wrapped and refrigerated for up to 4 hours.)

5 Meanwhile, make glaze: Bring all glaze ingredients to a simmer in a heavy, medium sized saucepan over medium heat, stirring to combine. Simmer over medium-low heat until slightly reduced, about 5 minutes. Let cool.

6 To prepare peaches: Toss peaches with butter in a medium bowl.

7 Return grill to medium (425°F) heat. Brush grill grate clean. Place unwrapped ribs on grill grate and cover grill. Cook, turning halfway through cooking, brushing occasionally with the glaze, until ribs are sizzling, about 6 minutes (or 8 to 10 minutes for refrigerated ribs.)

8 Add peaches to grill. Brush with glaze and continue grilling, turning occasionally, until peaches are heated through and seared and ribs are glazed, about 5 minutes more. Remove from grill.

9 Transfer ribs to a carving board and let stand for 5 minutes. Cut between bones into individual ribs. Transfer to a serving platter and add peaches. Season peaches with pepper. Serve hot.

CEDAR-PLANKED SALMON

MAIN COURSE

DF | GF | 🍷

with CUCUMBER SALSA

MAKES 8 SERVINGS

WINE SUGGESTION: NEW ZEALAND SAUVIGNON BLANC

Grilling fish on planks of untreated cedar is a popular cooking technique in the Pacific Northwest that has spread throughout the country. Served with a crisp cucumber salsa, this restaurant-style dish can be easily made at home.

YOU WILL NEED

CUCUMBER SALSA

3 large cucumbers

1 teaspoon kosher salt

1 green onion, including green parts, finely chopped

3 tablespoons minced fresh cilantro, basil, or flat-leaf parsley

3 tablespoons fresh lemon juice

1 jalapeño chile, seeded and minced

$\frac{1}{4}$ cup extra-virgin olive oil

2 tablespoons fresh lemon juice

One 3 $\frac{1}{2}$-pound trimmed salmon fillet

1 untreated cedar plank for grilling, soaked in water for 1 hour and drained

$\frac{1}{2}$ teaspoon salt

$\frac{1}{2}$ teaspoon freshly ground black pepper

1 To make salsa: Peel each cucumber and cut in half lengthwise. Using a dessert spoon, scoop out seeds. Cut cucumbers into $\frac{1}{2}$-inch cubes and place in a colander. Toss with salt. Let stand for 30 minutes. Rinse cucumbers well under cold running water, drain, and pat dry with paper towels. Mix cucumbers with green onion, cilantro, lemon juice, and jalapeño. Cover and refrigerate until chilled, at least 1 hour or up to 8 hours.

2 Whisk oil and lemon juice in a glass or ceramic dish just large enough to hold salmon. Add salmon and turn to coat with marinade. Let stand at room temperature for 30 minutes, no longer.

3 Prepare an outdoor grill for indirect cooking over medium (400°F) heat.

continued

4 Place drained cedar plank over hot side of grill. Heat, turning occasionally, until plank is smoking, about 4 minutes. Remove salmon from marinade, season with salt and pepper, and place on hot plank. Place plank over cooler (unlighted) side of the grill and cover. Grill until salmon has turned opaque on outside but has a rosy center when flaked with tip of a sharp knife, about 20 minutes. Using two large spatulas or a rimless baking sheet, transfer salmon to a long serving platter.

5 Cut salmon in half lengthwise, then crosswise into portions, and serve with cucumber salsa passed on side.

SALT

On paper, salt is salt, as it is always composed of sodium chloride. Yet salt comes in many different crystal shapes and even different colors. Some cooks taste differences in the various kinds of salt, too.

In this book, we use two kinds of salt, kosher and fine sea salt. Kosher salt has large, flat flakes that are easy to pinch with your fingertips. It can be either mined or made from saltwater, and it usually does not include additives. Fine sea salt is derived from seawater and evaporated into fine crystals that dissolve easily in batters and doughs, which is why we prefer it for baking.

Finishing salts are coarse-grained salt crystals that are best reserved for sprinkling over cooked food as a final touch just before serving. These salts—such as Hawaiian pink or black salts—often bear the color of the original rock used for mining.

>>‹‹

BEEF

Do you ever wonder why steaks served at fine steakhouses are tender and flavorful, while the steaks you buy at your standard supermarket are tough and dry? Rest assured, it's not your grilling skills!

To create an unforgettable meal, you must start with the best beef you can buy. At The Fresh Market, we offer only premium beef that is aged to perfection and richly marbled with flavor.

The Fresh Market's Premium Choice beef includes only the top 10 percent of all beef in the United States. This marbling standard produces the juiciest, most savory beef imaginable. Add our aging requirements and steak-trim standards, and our Premium Choice is regarded as the very best beef in the country!

Our TFM Hereford Beef is selected solely on its genetic breed. Hereford, one of the three original breeds of cattle (along with Angus and Shorthorn), is noted for its outstanding culinary qualities. The Hereford breed produces meat that is generally leaner and more flavorful, and yet wonderfully tender.

And you can rest assured that our ground beef meets the same strict quality standards as our other cuts. We guarantee that our beef is ground fresh daily from whole roasts and steak trimmings and is sold only on the day it is ground. Our butchers never use "pink slime" (off cuts of beef) to extend our product. We provide a far superior and safer product, and we can't imagine it any other way.

GRILLED RIB-EYE STEAK

with COFFEEHOUSE RUB

MAIN COURSE

MAKES 4 SERVINGS

WINE SUGGESTION: MALBEC

Rib-eye steak grills up juicy and tender because of its intramuscular fat, which causes flare-ups as it melts and drips on the coals. Grill it with the lid closed to reduce the amount of oxygen that feeds the flames, and you will be fine. The espresso rub may sound unusual, but it works beautifully.

YOU WILL NEED

RUB

1 tablespoon coarsely ground espresso beans

2 teaspoons chili powder

2 teaspoons light brown sugar

1 tablespoon minced fresh oregano, or 1 teaspoon dried oregano

1 teaspoon kosher salt

$1/2$ teaspoon freshly ground black pepper

$1/4$ teaspoon granulated garlic

$1/4$ teaspoon granulated onion

Four 12-ounce rib-eye steaks, cut 1 inch thick

Extra-virgin olive oil for brushing

1 To make rub: Combine all rub ingredients in a small bowl. Brush steaks with oil and season with rub. Let stand at room temperature for 30 minutes.

2 Prepare an outdoor grill for direct cooking over high (500°F) heat.

3 Brush grill grate clean. Place steaks on grill and close lid. Cook until steaks are browned on bottom, about 3 minutes. Flip steaks over and cook until other side is browned, 3 to 4 minutes more for medium-rare. It is difficult to test steak with an instant-read thermometer, so judge by touch (see note) or by cutting into steak to check color. Remove from grill and let stand for 3 minutes before serving.

JUDGING DONENESS BY TOUCH: Some steaks, burgers, and fillets are too thin to get a correct reading with a thermometer, but you can test doneness by touch. Press meat in its thickest part with your forefinger. If it is rare, it will feel squishy. Meat cooked to medium will have some resilience, and well-done meat will feel firm. Remove meat from grill just before you think it has reached its optimum temperature and let it stand at room temperature for 3 to 5 minutes before serving.

Tian is a beloved entrée in Provençal French cooking, a kind of crustless quiche that is often bolstered with rice to make it more filling. While just about any cooked vegetable can be used, here rainbow chard and zucchini make the dish perfect for summer brunch. Chard is always sandy, so wash it very well to be sure to remove any grit. Serve the tian with grilled or sautéed sausages and a big green salad to fill out the menu.

YOU WILL NEED

1 pound rainbow chard, well washed, leaves and stems cut crosswise into $1/2$-inch-thick strips

$1/2$ cup Arborio rice

2 tablespoons extra-virgin olive oil

2 zucchini, trimmed and cut into $1/4$-inch-thick rounds

1 large yellow onion, chopped

2 garlic cloves, minced

4 large eggs

$3/4$ teaspoon kosher salt

$1/4$ teaspoon freshly ground black pepper

2 cups whole milk

$1/2$ cup (2 ounces) freshly grated Parmigiano-Reggiano

2 tablespoons dried bread crumbs

1 Bring a large saucepan of lightly salted water to a boil over high heat. Add chard and cook just until tender, about 3 minutes. Rinse under cold running water and drain. Let cool enough to handle. A handful at a time, squeeze excess liquid from chard. Coarsely chop chard.

2 Meanwhile, bring a medium saucepan of lightly salted water to a boil over high heat. Add rice and cook, uncovered, until tender, about 18 minutes. Drain in a fine-mesh sieve and rinse under cold running water; drain again.

3 Heat oil in a large sauté pan over medium heat. Add zucchini and cook, stirring occasionally, until it begins to soften, about 3 minutes. Add onion and cook, stirring occasionally, until vegetables are tender, about 5 minutes. Stir in garlic and cook until fragrant, about 1 minute. Set aside and let cool slightly. (Zucchini mixture, chard, and rice can be combined, covered, and refrigerated for up to 1 day.)

④ Preheat oven to 350°F. Lightly oil a 9-by-13-inch baking dish. In a large bowl, whisk eggs, salt, and pepper until combined. Gradually whisk in milk, then Parmigiano-Reggiano. Stir in zucchini mixture, chopped chard, and rice. Spread in baking dish and sprinkle with crumbs.

⑤ Bake until set in center, about 30 minutes. Let stand at room temperature for 10 minutes before serving warm or at room temperature. (The tian can be made 1 day ahead, cooled, covered with aluminum foil, and refrigerated. Let come to room temperature to serve, or cover and bake in a preheated 350°F oven until reheated, about 20 minutes.)

SUMMER SQUASH

Squash is not really a vegetable, but the fruit of a vine. Summer squash may be the most versatile of hot-weather produce. It can be grilled, sautéed, stuffed and roasted, served raw in salad, simmered into soup, and even stirred into batter and baked as a dessert. In Mexican cuisine, the flowers are made into a soup, and Italian cooks fill and fry the blooms. Eating the flowers before they turn into squash is an effective way to control the size of the crop, as the vines are famously fruitful and can take over a garden. Having many cooking options is a boon in August when summer squash is ubiquitous and reasonably priced.

Summer squash, with its thin peel and tender flesh, is the direct opposite of the hearty, thick-skinned winter squash. The most common summer squash are zucchini and yellow squash, and you may also find other varieties for sale, such as the puck-shaped pattypan and baby squash. Just give summer squash a light scrub under cold running water to rinse away any clinging grit, and it will be ready to star in any number of warm-weather dishes.

≫❦≪

ZUCCHINI PIE

with POLENTA CRUST

MAIN COURSE

MAKES 4—6 SERVINGS

A vegetarian member of the deep-dish pie family, this version has a cheesy polenta layer for its top crust. For a spicier version, substitute cilantro for the basil and add 1 seeded and minced jalapeño chile to the onion mixture.

YOU WILL NEED

FILLING

2 tablespoons extra-virgin olive oil

2 pounds zucchini, trimmed and cut into $1/2$-inch dice

1 large yellow onion, chopped

1 red bell pepper, seeded, deribbed, and cut into $1/2$-inch dice

2 garlic cloves, minced

One 14$1/2$-ounce can diced tomatoes with juice

2 tablespoons minced fresh basil

Kosher salt and freshly ground black pepper

POLENTA CRUST

1 cup yellow cornmeal

2 cups water

$3/4$ teaspoon salt

$1/4$ teaspoon freshly ground black pepper

1 $1/2$ cups (6 ounces) shredded fontina or white Cheddar cheese

1 Preheat oven to 350°F. Lightly oil a 9-inch deep-dish pie pan.

2 To make filling: Heat oil in a large skillet over medium-high heat. Add zucchini, onion, bell pepper, and garlic. Cook, stirring occasionally, until zucchini is tender and lightly browned, about 15 minutes. Add tomatoes and their juices and bring to a boil. Reduce heat to medium-low and simmer until tomato juices thicken, about 5 minutes. Stir in basil. Season with salt and pepper. Spread evenly in pie pan.

3 Meanwhile, make crust: Whisk cornmeal with 1 cup of water in a small bowl. Combine remaining 1 cup water, salt, and pepper in a medium saucepan. Whisk in cornmeal mixture and bring to a boil over high heat. Reduce heat to medium-low and let bubble for 2 minutes. Stir in 1 cup of fontina. Spread over zucchini to within 1 inch of the edge of pan plate, which will allow the filling to peek out after baking. Sprinkle remaining $1/2$ cup cheese on top. Place pie pan on a baking sheet and bake until edges of crust are lightly browned, about 25 minutes. Let stand for 5 minutes, then serve hot.

GRILLED EGGPLANT

& FONTINA SANDWICHES

MAIN COURSE

MAKES 6 SANDWICHES

WINE SUGGESTION: CHIANTI

Eggplant has a substantial, almost meaty texture that makes it great for sandwiches. These are hot from the grill, layered with melting cheese, spicy arugula, and tapenade. (You can also use a broiler to cook the eggplant and toast the bread.) Crusty sourdough is a must in this recipe.

 YOU WILL NEED

1 large (1 ½ pounds) eggplant, top trimmed

Kosher salt

Extra-virgin olive oil for brushing

6 ounces fontina cheese, sliced and cut into 12 equal pieces

12 slices crusty sourdough bread (cut from a wide loaf)

1 cup olive tapenade

1 bunch arugula, stemmed

1 Using a serrated knife, cut eggplant crosswise into 12 slices about ½ inch thick. Place eggplant in a colander. Sprinkle with 1 tablespoon of salt and toss. Let stand in a sink to drain for 1 hour. Rinse eggplant under cold water. Pat dry with paper towels.

2 Meanwhile, prepare an outdoor grill for direct cooking over medium-high (400°F) heat.

3 Brush eggplant rounds on both sides with oil. Brush grill grate clean. Place eggplant on grill and close grill lid. Cook until eggplant is browned on bottom, about 4 minutes. Turn and cook until eggplant is tender, about 4 minutes more. Top each eggplant round with a piece of fontina. Transfer to a platter. (Residual heat will melt cheese.)

4 Place bread slices on grill and grill, turning once, until toasted, about 1 minute. Transfer to platter.

5 For each sandwich, spread two bread slices with tapenade. Place two eggplant slices on one piece of bread and top with a few arugula leaves. Top with second piece of bread and cut in half. Serve at once.

RATATOUILLE CASSEROLE

WINE SUGGESTION: FRENCH ROSE

Here's the scenario: It's a hot summer day, and you have a kitchen full of produce begging to be cooked, but you cannot bear to turn on the stove. There is a solution: Turn your outside grill into an oven by using indirect heat (see page 70). This colorful dish of zucchini, yellow squash, and tomatoes is bound to become a favorite.

YOU WILL NEED

1 globe eggplant (about 1 1/4 pounds), top trimmed

Kosher salt

5 tablespoons extra-virgin olive oil

2 yellow onions, chopped

4 garlic cloves, minced

2 teaspoons minced fresh thyme

1/2 teaspoon red pepper flakes

1 zucchini, trimmed and cut into 1/2-inch-thick rounds

1 yellow squash, trimmed and cut into 1/2-inch-thick rounds

4 plum (Roma) tomatoes, cut into 1/2-inch-thick rounds

1/4 cup freshly grated Parmigiano-Reggiano

1/4 cup dried bread crumbs

1 Cut eggplant into 1/2-inch-thick rounds. Cut larger slices in half crosswise to make half-moon shapes. Transfer to a colander, sprinkle with 1 tablespoon of salt, and toss well. Let stand in a sink for about 1 hour to drain excess juice. Rinse well and pat dry.

2 Prepare an outdoor grill for indirect cooking over medium (425°F) heat. Lightly oil a 9-by-13-inch baking dish, preferably enameled cast iron, ceramic, or earthenware.

3 Heat 2 tablespoons of oil in a large skillet over medium heat. Add onions and cook, stirring occasionally, until translucent, about 5 minutes. Stir in garlic and cook until fragrant, about 1 minute. Spread onion mixture in baking dish.

④ In a small bowl, mix thyme with 1 ½ teaspoons of salt and pepper flakes. Standing vegetable slices upright in rows, alternate eggplant, zucchini, yellow squash, and tomatoes in the dish, packing them fairly tightly. Season evenly with thyme mixture and drizzle with remaining 3 tablespoons oil. Cover tightly with aluminum foil.

⑤ Place baking dish over cool area of grill. Cover grill and cook until vegetables are softened, about 1 hour. Remove foil and sprinkle vegetables with Parmigiano-Reggiano and bread crumbs. Return to grill, close grill lid, and continue cooking until vegetables are very tender and crumb mixture is browned (cover dish loosely with aluminum foil if the crumbs are browned before vegetables are done), 15 to 20 minutes. Let stand at room temperature for 20 minutes to serve warm or at room temperature.

EGGPLANT

Eggplant must be cooked to reveal its delicious flavor and melting texture. Traditionally, globe eggplant was salted to release its bitter juices, but modern varieties are sweeter and salting is now done to soften the flesh and keep it from absorbing too much liquid during cooking. (Fried globe eggplant can soak up an alarming amount of oil, which results in a very heavy dish.)

Most American cooks are familiar with the purple-black, thick-skinned globe eggplant, which can grow to an impressive football size. Japanese eggplants are smaller, with an elongated shape and thin skin; they do not need to be salted. You may also see white or round eggplants. Buy heavy eggplants with smooth, unmarred skin and fresh-looking green caps. Although they look sturdy, eggplants are surprisingly perishable and should be stored in the refrigerator. Carbon steel will leave a dark stain on eggplant, so use a stainless-steel or ceramic knife for prepping.

GRILLED WHITE PIZZA

with ZUCCHINI

MAKES 4—6 SERVINGS

WINE SUGGESTION: CHARDONNAY

For some cooks, grilling has surpassed baking as the preferred method for making pizza. Don't worry about timing, because the pizza crusts can be pre-grilled, then finished an hour or so later with the summery toppings of plum tomatoes, zucchini, and basil. The dough recipe uses instant yeast and is very easy to make. One trick to keep in mind: Grill pizza over medium, not high, heat, to have more control over the process.

YOU WILL NEED

DOUGH

3 cups unbleached all-purpose flour

2 tablespoons extra-virgin olive oil

2 1/4 teaspoons instant yeast (also called bread machine or quick-rising yeast)

1 1/2 teaspoons fine sea salt

1 cup cold water

1/4 cup extra-virgin olive oil, plus more for brushing

2 garlic cloves, minced

2 large zucchini, trimmed and cut lengthwise into 1/4-inch-thick strips

Kosher salt and freshly ground black pepper

1 pound fresh mozzarella, cut into 1/2-inch-thick slices, and then cut into 2-inch-wide pieces

2 ripe plum (Roma) tomatoes, seeded and cut into 1/2-inch dice

1 cup whole milk or part-skim ricotta cheese

4 tablespoons coarsely chopped fresh basil

Red pepper flakes, for serving

1 To make dough with a food processor: Pulse flour, oil, yeast, and salt together in a food processor. With machine running, add enough of water to make a dough that rides on top of blade and process for 45 seconds. (To make dough by hand, stir water, oil, and yeast together in a large bowl. Stir in 1 cup of flour and salt. Gradually stir in enough of remaining flour to make a dough that can't be stirred. Turn out onto a floured work surface and knead by hand, adding more flour as needed, to make a soft, supple dough, about 10 minutes.)

continued

② Gather dough into a ball. Oil a medium bowl, place dough in bowl, and turn to coat. Cover bowl tightly with plastic wrap. Let stand in a warm, draft-free place until dough doubles in volume (a fingertip inserted $1/2$ inch into dough will leave an impression intact for at least 10 seconds), about $1^1/_4$ hours. (Dough can be punched down, covered, and refrigerated for up to 1 day. Remove from refrigerator 1 hour before shaping.)

③ Prepare an outdoor grill for direct cooking over medium (350° to 400°F) heat.

④ Brush grill grate clean. Combine $1/4$ cup oil and garlic in a small bowl. Brush zucchini with some of garlic oil. Arrange zucchini on grill, perpendicular to grids, and close grill lid. Grill, turning once, until crisp-tender and seared with grill marks, about 5 minutes. Transfer to a plate. Let cool slightly, then coarsely chop zucchini. Season with salt and pepper.

⑤ Cut two 12-inch-square sheets of parchment paper. Divide dough in half and shape each portion into a ball. Cover with plastic wrap and let rest for 10 minutes. Working with one ball of dough at a time on a lightly floured work surface, roll, pat, and stretch dough into a 12-inch-diameter round. If dough retracts, cover with plastic wrap, let stand for 5 minutes, then try again. Transfer dough to parchment paper and brush with olive oil. Stack dough rounds (still on parchment) on a large baking sheet and cover with a dampened kitchen towel.

⑥ Brush grill grate clean again. Flip one dough round, oiled side down, onto grill and close grill lid. Grill until dough is set and underside is lightly browned, about 3 minutes. Remove parchment paper. Using a wide spatula, turn dough and grill other side until lightly browned. Transfer to a platter. Repeat with other dough round. (Pizza rounds can be prepared up to 2 hours ahead and stored, uncovered, at room temperature. When ready to finish, prepare grill again for medium direct heat.)

⑦ Return a pizza round to grill, cover, and cook until warmed on bottom, about 1 minute. Turn pizza and top with half of mozzarella. Scatter half of zucchini and tomatoes over mozzarella, followed by dollops of half of ricotta. Cover and grill until pizza is heated through and cheese is melted, about 3 minutes. Transfer to a baking sheet and tent with aluminum foil to keep warm while grilling remaining pizza round with remaining mozzarella, zucchini, tomatoes, and ricotta. Drizzle each pizza with half of remaining garlic oil and sprinkle with half of basil and red pepper. Cut into wedges and serve hot.

GRILLED PASTA SAUCE

with TOMATOES & BASIL

WINE SUGGESTION: VALPOLICELLA

Take advantage of summer tomatoes with this mouthwatering sauce that is cooked entirely outdoors. (If your gas grill has a side burner, you can even boil the water for the pasta outside, too.) The meatless sauce is a good match for thin, delicate pasta, such as capellini. If the weather is cool enough and you can cook indoors, see the variation for roasting.

YOU WILL NEED

SAUCE

2 1/2 pounds plum (Roma) tomatoes, cored and halved lengthwise

2 tablespoons extra-virgin olive oil

Kosher salt and freshly ground black pepper

2 garlic cloves, minced

1/4 cup packed fresh basil leaves

1 pound capellini (angel hair) pasta

3 tablespoons extra-virgin olive oil

Freshly grated Parmigiano-Reggiano, for serving

1. Prepare an outdoor grill for indirect cooking over medium (400°F) heat.

2. Lightly oil a 9-by-13-inch baking dish. Arrange tomatoes, cut side up, in pan—they will be crowded. Drizzle with oil and season with 1 teaspoon salt and 1/4 teaspoon pepper. Place on cool side of grill and close grill lid. Cook until tomatoes are lightly browned around edges and very tender, about 1 1/4 hours.

3. In batches, pulse tomatoes, garlic, and basil in a food processor until coarsely chopped. Season with salt and pepper. Pour into a large serving bowl.

4. Meanwhile, bring a large pot of salted water to a boil over high heat. Add pasta and cook according to package directions. Drain and transfer hot pasta to bowl with sauce. Drizzle with oil and toss. Serve with Parmigiano-Reggiano passed on side.

OVEN-ROASTED METHOD: Arrange tomatoes, cut side up, in oiled large rimmed baking sheet. Season with salt and pepper. Roast in preheated 400°F oven until very tender, about 45 minutes. Proceed as directed.

FARFALLE WITH ARUGULA

& SAUSAGE

PASTA

MAKES 4—6 SERVINGS

WINE SUGGESTION: PINOT GRIGIO

Arugula can be spicy in a salad, but its heat is reduced by cooking. Like other greens, it wilts dramatically, so make this rustic but sophisticated pasta when the summer crop of arugula is plentiful. This pasta is moistened with olive oil, and the better your oil the more delicious the final dish will be.

YOU WILL NEED

1 pound arugula

5 tablespoons extra-virgin olive oil, preferably estate quality

1 yellow onion, chopped

2 garlic cloves, minced

4 ounces sweet Italian pork or turkey sausage, casing removed

$^1/_4$ teaspoon red pepper flakes

1 pound farfalle (bow-tie pasta)

$^1/_2$ cup (2 ounces) freshly grated Parmigiano-Reggiano, plus more for serving

Kosher salt

1 Discard tough stems from arugula. Wash arugula well in a large sink of cold water. Lift arugula from water and shake off excess, but do not spin dry.

2 Heat 1 tablespoon of oil in a large skillet over medium heat. Add onion and cook until softened but not browned, about 3 minutes. Add garlic and stir until fragrant, about 1 minute. Add sausage and pepper flakes and cook, breaking meat into small pieces with side of a spoon, until meat loses its pink color, about 4 minutes. In four or five additions, add arugula, stirring until one batch wilts before adding another. Cover and reduce heat to medium-low. Simmer until arugula is tender, about 5 minutes.

3 Meanwhile, bring a large pot of lightly salted water to a boil over high heat. Add pasta and cook until al dente according to package directions.

4 Scoop out and reserve $^1/_2$ cup of pasta cooking water. Drain pasta and return it to pot. Add arugula mixture and remaining 4 tablespoons olive oil and mix well. Add $^1/_2$ cup Parmigiano-Reggiano and toss again, adding enough of reserved cooking water to moisten pasta. Season with salt. Serve at once, with additional cheese passed at table.

ICE CREAM SUNDAES *with*

GRILLED PINEAPPLE

& CARAMEL-RUM SAUCE

DESSERT

GF | V

MAKES 8 SERVINGS

Any warm dessert with ice cream automatically gets extra points. The interplay between hot and cold, tangy and sweet makes this treat extra special. Pineapple is available year-round, but is particularly abundant in the summer. A quick trip to the grill or broiler caramelizes its juices and brings out its sweetness.

YOU WILL NEED

CARAMEL-RUM SAUCE

1/4 cup water

1 cup sugar

2 cups heavy cream, heated

2 tablespoons golden or dark rum

1/2 teaspoon vanilla extract

1 ripe pineapple, pared, cored, and cut crosswise into 8 slices

Canola or vegetable oil for brushing

1 quart vanilla ice cream

1 To make sauce: Pour water into a heavy, medium-sized saucepan. Add sugar and cook over high heat, stirring just until sugar melts. Cook without stirring, occasionally swirling melted sugar in pan and brushing down any crystals that form on sides of pan with a pastry brush, until sugar has caramelized to a dark copper-brown, 3 to 5 minutes.

2 Slowly pour in hot cream; mixture will bubble up, so be very careful. Boil, stirring often, until sauce has reduced to 2 cups, about 3 minutes. Remove from heat and stir in rum and vanilla. Let cool to room temperature.

3 Prepare an outdoor grill for direct cooking over medium (350°F) heat.

4 Brush pineapple slices with oil. Brush grill grate clean. Place pineapple slices on grill and close grill lid. Grill pineapple until grill-marked on bottom, about 3 minutes. Turn pineapple and cook until second side is grill-marked, 3 minutes more. Transfer pineapple to a cutting board and coarsely chop into bite-sized pieces. Let cool for 5 to 10 minutes.

5 Scoop ice cream into dessert bowls. Top with warm pineapple and its juices, then with caramel sauce. Serve at once.

FRESH BLUEBERRY TART

Here's a fancy, show-off fruit tart that you can practically make with your eyes closed. The almonds in the dough enhance the flavor of the plump blueberries. A glaze of fruit preserves gives the fruit a gorgeous sheen. Serve it with a scoop of ice cream or a dollop of crème fraîche.

YOU WILL NEED

Almond Pastry Dough (page 49)

FILLING

1 tablespoon cornstarch

³/₄ cup water

Three 6-ounce containers fresh blueberries (4 cups)

¹/₂ cup sugar

Grated zest of 1 lemon

2 tablespoons fresh lemon juice

2 tablespoons unsalted butter

¹/₂ cup blueberry or raspberry preserves, for glaze

2 tablespoons sliced almonds, toasted (see page 111), for garnish

Confectioners' sugar, for dusting

1 Preheat oven to 375°F. Lightly butter a 9-inch tart pan with a removable bottom. Gather dough and press evenly into pan using your fingertips, being sure that sides and bottom meet at a sharp 90-degree angle (think of how a floor meets a wall). Pierce crust all over with a fork and cover the pan with plastic wrap. Freeze until firm, 20 to 30 minutes.

2 Unwrap crust and line with lightly buttered aluminum foil, buttered side down. Fill pan with pastry weights or dried beans. Place on a baking sheet. Bake until crust looks set, about 15 minutes. Carefully remove foil and weights and continue baking until crust is golden brown, about 15 more minutes. Let cool completely on a wire rack.

3 To make filling: Sprinkle cornstarch over $1/4$ cup of water in a small bowl and whisk to dissolve; set aside. Bring 2 cups of blueberries, remaining $1/2$ cup water, sugar, lemon zest, and lemon juice to a boil in a medium saucepan over high heat, stirring often. Reduce heat to medium-low and simmer until berries are soft, about 5 minutes. Stir in dissolved cornstarch mixture and cook just until juices thicken, about 30 seconds. Do not overcook. Remove from heat and stir in butter. Cool until lukewarm but still pourable.

4 Spread filling evenly in cooled tart shell. Arrange remaining fresh blueberries over filling. In a small saucepan, bring preserves to a boil. Strain through a sieve, pressing on solids with back of a large spoon. Brush strained hot preserves over berries. Sprinkle a 1-inch ring of almonds around edge of filling. Let cool completely.

5 Cover loosely with plastic wrap and refrigerate until filling is chilled and set, at least 2 hours. (Tart can be prepared up to 8 hours ahead.) Remove sides of tart pan. (The easiest way to do this is to place pan on a large can and let side drop down like a ring around can.) Dust top of tart with confectioners' sugar. Serve chilled or at room temperature.

BING CHERRY GALETTE

It is good to know how to make a galette, a free-form tart that can be whipped up in minutes to take advantage of whatever irresistible fresh fruit you have at hand. When there is a bowl of Bing cherries in your kitchen, transform some of them into this galette and serve it warm with a scoop of vanilla ice cream. Cookie crumbs (or you can substitute vanilla-flavored muffin or cake crumbs) absorb the cherry juices during baking to keep the pastry crisp.

 YOU WILL NEED

DOUGH

1 cup unbleached all-purpose flour, plus more for rolling dough

2 tablespoons sugar

Pinch of kosher salt

1/2 cup (1 stick) cold unsalted butter, cut into 1/2-inch cubes

2 tablespoons ice water

1 egg yolk

1/3 cup vanilla wafer crumbs (wafers crushed in a food processor)

12 ounces Bing cherries, pitted (about 1 1/2 cups)

1 tablespoon sugar

2 tablespoons sliced almonds

2 tablespoons cold unsalted butter, cut into 1/4-inch cubes

1 To make dough: In a food processor, pulse together 1 cup flour, sugar, and salt. Add butter and pulse about 10 times until dough resembles coarse meal with some pea-sized pieces of butter. In a small bowl, mix together ice water and egg yolk. With machine running, add egg yolk mixture and process just until it clumps together. (To make by hand: Mix together flour, sugar, and salt in a medium bowl. Using a pastry blender, cut in butter until mixture is crumbly. Stir in enough of egg yolk mixture until dough clumps together.) Gather dough into a thick disk and wrap in plastic wrap. Refrigerate for at least 15 minutes or up to 1 hour.

2 Preheat oven to 400°F. Line a baking sheet with parchment paper.

3 Roll dough on a lightly floured work surface into a 12- to 13-inch-diameter round. Spread cookie crumbs in a thin 9-inch-diameter layer over pastry. Top with cherries and sprinkle with sugar. Fold over edges of dough, loosely pleating it as needed. Scatter almonds over cherries and dot with butter.

continued

4 Bake for 10 minutes. Reduce heat to 375°F and continue baking until cherry juices are bubbling and pastry is golden brown, about 20 minutes more. Let cool on baking sheet for 10 minutes. Slide off parchment paper onto a large plate and serve warm or at room temperature.

STONE FRUITS

Apricots, peaches, nectarines, plums, and cherries are among the most anticipated of all warm-weather produce. The juicy flesh of each fruit encompasses a hard pit, also called a stone. Cling varieties have flesh that attaches itself to the pit. If the pit is loose and easily removed from the flesh, the variety is a freestone fruit. Most early-season peaches, for example, are cling, with the freestones showing up later in the season.

Each fruit has a number of variations. The best eating cherries are the deep red Bing and the yellow-blushed Rainier and Queen Anne. You will find a range of peach types throughout the summer, including the standard yellow peach (even if it is more golden than yellow), the squat donut, and the pale-fleshed white peach. The nectarine is a close cousin of the peach, without fuzz on its skin. Plums are another prolific fruit with many types, from the magenta Santa Rosa to the black-skinned plum and the frosted-blue-purple Italian. Apricots are fairly standard, although interspecies, such as the plumcot (a plum-apricot cross), aprium (the same, with more apricot), and pluot (mostly plum with a hint of apricot flavor) are showing up more often. Always keep stone fruits at room temperature, and refrigerate them only when you want to slow down the natural ripening process.

While stone fruits are often the basis for wonderful baked goods, one of the true joys of summer is eating them in their unadorned glory. Serve them European-style in a bowl of ice for the simplest of all desserts.

❯❯❮❮

PEACH-PECAN SHORTCAKE

Warm shortcake, layered with juicy peaches and topped with whipped cream, is detectable on a warm summer day. There are many keys to shortcake perfection, including using a low-gluten mix of two flours, mixing the dough with a light hand, and using the best fresh fruit.

 YOU WILL NEED

PEACHES

3 pounds ripe peaches, pitted and sliced

1/3 cup packed light brown sugar, or as needed

SHORTCAKE

1 cup cake flour

1 cup unbleached all-purpose flour

1/3 cup granulated sugar

1 tablespoon baking powder

1/4 teaspoon salt

1/2 cup coarsely chopped pecans

1/2 cup (1 stick) cold unsalted butter, cut into 1/2-inch cubes

2/3 cup whole milk, or as needed

Whipped Cream (page 45)

1 At least 4 hours before serving, prepare peaches. Stir peaches and brown sugar together in a medium bowl. Cover and refrigerate until peaches give off their juices, at least 4 hours or up to 8 hours.

2 To make shortcake: Preheat oven to 375°F. Lightly butter and flour a 9-inch cake pan and tap out excess flour.

3 Pulse cake and all-purpose flours, sugar, baking powder, and salt in a food processor to combine. Add pecans and pulse about 10 times until pecans are very finely chopped but not a powder. Add butter and pulse 8 to 10 times until mixture resembles coarse crumbs with a few pea-sized pieces of butter. Transfer to a medium bowl. Stirring with a fork, mix in enough of milk to make a soft dough. (To make by hand, chop pecans until very fine. Using a whisk, stir flours, sugar, and salt together. Stir in pecans. Using a pastry blender, cut in butter, then stir in milk.) Knead dough in bowl a few times, just until smooth. Do not overwork dough. Pat dough evenly into cake pan.

continued

4 Bake until shortcake is golden brown, 25 to 30 minutes. Transfer pan to a wire rack and let shortcake cool for 10 minutes, then remove from pan. Let cool until warm, about 15 minutes. (Shortcake can be made up to 8 hours ahead, cooled, wrapped in aluminum foil, and stored at room temperature. Reheat in a preheated 350°F oven until warm, about 10 minutes.)

5 Using a serrated knife, cut warm shortcake into 8 wedges. Place each shortcake wedge in a dessert bowl. Top with equal amounts of peaches and a large spoonful of whipped cream. Serve at once.

MELON & LIME ICE POPS

Even households without kids should have a set of plastic ice-pop molds. Is there anything that says summer more clearly than cooling off in the shade while eating a fruit pop? Use your favorite melon—honeydew, cantaloupe, and watermelon are all good—just as long as it is very ripe and sweet. The number of pops, of course, depends on the capacity of the molds, which average about ¼ cup each.

YOU WILL NEED

3 cups cubed ripe melon

½ cup sugar, preferably superfine

Grated zest of 1 lime

2 tablespoons fresh lime juice

Wooden treat sticks (optional)

1 Have ready 8 ice-pop molds. Purée melon in a food processor or blender and measure purée. You should have a scant 2 cups.

2 Return purée to food processor and process with sugar, lime zest, and juice until sugar dissolves. Divide purée among ice-pop molds, cover each mold with its lid, and add wooden sticks, if using.

3 Freeze until pops are solid, about 4 hours. (Pops can be stored in freezer for up to 1 week.) To serve, rinse pop molds under lukewarm water and remove pops from molds. Serve at once.

BUILDER

SOUP & SALADS

DF · VEGAN · VEGETARIAN — Carrot Slaw with Miso Vinaigrette 109

DF · GF · VEGAN · VEGETARIAN — Fuyu Persimmon Salad with Ginger Vinaigrette 111

GF · VEGETARIAN — Rutabaga & Apple Bisque 112

MAIN COURSES

Pork Chops with Creamy Chanterelle Sauce 113

GF — Parmigiano Tilapia with Fennel & Potatoes 115

Classic Roast Turkey with Rosemary Gravy 117

PASTAS & SIDE DISHES

GF · VEGETARIAN — Celery Root & Potato Purée with Gruyère 121

DF · VEGAN · VEGETARIAN — Moroccan Roasted Vegetables on Cilantro Couscous 122

Fettuccine with Pancetta & Brussels Sprouts 125

Penne with Cauliflower & Sage 127

Fall Vegetable Stuffing with Sausage 128

DF · GF · VEGAN · VEGETARIAN — Gingered Cranberry Sauce 130

DESSERTS

VEGETARIAN — Creamy Apple Crostata 131

VEGETARIAN — Double-Crust Fig Tart 133

VEGETARIAN — Autumn Plum Cake 137

DF · VEGETARIAN — Sweet Potato Cake with Orange Icing 139

VEGETARIAN — Pumpkin Jumbles 141

DF ‖ DAIRY-FREE   GF ‖ GLUTEN-FREE   ✌ ‖ VEGAN   🛡 ‖ VEGETARIAN

FALL

FALL SIGNALS THE WINDING DOWN

OF THE GROWING SEASON AND PROVIDES
US WITH FOOD TO STORE DURING THE
COMING COLD MONTHS.

*Root vegetables, such as carrots, celery root, and
rutabagas, sustained our ancestors, but now we
eat them for their deliciously earthy flavors. At
the beginning of the season, figs and Italian
plums are holdovers from summer, and then
make room for apples and persimmons in the
fruit bowl. The Thanksgiving celebration, with a
beautiful turkey at center stage, symbolizes the
harvest season.*

· CARROT SLAW ·

with MISO VINAIGRETTE

SALAD

MAKES 4 SERVINGS

The complex flavor of miso makes a fine salad dressing for green salads, composed salads, and vegetable slaws like this one. The combination of salty miso and sweet carrots is an inspired mix.

YOU WILL NEED

MISO VINAIGRETTE

2 tablespoons rice vinegar

1 tablespoon light (white or yellow) miso

½ teaspoon Japanese soy sauce or tamari sauce

1 small garlic clove, chopped

½ cup vegetable oil

1 pound carrots, peeled

1 green onion, including green parts, finely chopped

Kosher salt and freshly ground black pepper

Sesame seeds, for garnish

1 To make vinaigrette: Pulse vinegar, miso, soy sauce, and garlic in a blender to combine. With machine running, gradually pour oil through top vent to emulsify.

2 Shred carrots in a food processor with coarse shredding blade or a V-slicer. Transfer to a medium bowl and add green onion and vinaigrette. Toss gently. Season with salt and pepper. Serve at once, topping each serving with a sprinkle of sesame seeds.

FUYU PERSIMMON SALAD

with GINGER VINAIGRETTE

The beautiful, fiery orange Fuyu is the persimmon to use for salad. Squat and round, with a crisp texture and a honeyed apricot-like flavor, it doesn't need to be ripened like its cousin, the plumper Hachiya variety. In this salad, the fruit's sweetness is balanced by a zesty fresh-ginger dressing.

YOU WILL NEED

VINAIGRETTE

One 3-inch piece unpeeled fresh ginger

2 tablespoons minced shallots

2 tablespoons rice wine vinegar

1 teaspoon sugar

1/4 teaspoon kosher salt

1/8 teaspoon freshly ground black pepper

1/2 cup vegetable oil

1 tablespoon Asian sesame oil

6 ounces baby salad greens

2 firm Fuyu, cut into 1/4-inch wedges

1/2 cup pecan halves, toasted (see note) and coarsely chopped

1 To make vinaigrette: Shred ginger on large holes of a box grater. A handful at a time, squeeze ginger over a medium bowl to extract the juice. You should have about 2 tablespoons juice. Add shallots, vinegar, sugar, salt, and pepper. Gradually whisk in vegetable oil, followed by sesame oil. (Vinaigrette can be covered and refrigerated for up to 1 day. Whisk well before using.)

2 Combine salad greens, persimmons, and pecans in a large bowl. Add vinaigrette and toss well. Serve at once.

TOASTING NUTS: Spread nuts on a rimmed baking sheet. Bake in a preheated 350°F oven, stirring occasionally, until fragrant, about 10 minutes. Let cool completely.

RUTABAGA & APPLE BISQUE

SOUP

GF | V

MAKES 6–8 SERVINGS

Rutabaga, which can grow to the size of a cantaloupe, is sometimes called yellow turnip or swede and has an applied thick wax coating, which helps to keep it edible for months. It shows up around Thanksgiving, because mashed rutabagas are a must-have on some Turkey Day menus. Paired with sweet apples to tame its peppery, earthy flavor, rutabaga also makes an excellent soup. Substitute vegetable broth for the chicken broth to make a delicious vegetarian and gluten-free dish.

YOU WILL NEED

3 tablespoons unsalted butter

²/₃ cup minced shallots

2 ¹/₂ pounds rutabagas (yellow turnips), peeled and cut into 1-inch cubes

5 ¹/₂ cups reduced-sodium chicken broth or vegetable broth

3 Granny Smith apples, peeled, cored, and cut into ¹/₂-inch dice

¹/₂ cup heavy cream, plus more for drizzling

1 ¹/₂ teaspoons minced fresh thyme, or ¹/₂ teaspoon dried thyme

Kosher salt and freshly ground black pepper

1 In a large saucepan, melt 2 tablespoons of butter over medium heat. Add shallots and cook, stirring often, until tender, about 3 minutes. Add rutabagas and stir well. Add broth and bring to a boil over high heat. Reduce heat to medium-low. Cover and simmer until rutabagas are tender, about 45 minutes.

2 Meanwhile, in a large nonstick skillet, melt remaining 1 tablespoon butter over medium-high heat until foam subsides. Add apples and cook, stirring occasionally, until lightly browned, about 5 minutes. Transfer about one-third of apples to a bowl and reserve to use as garnish.

3 Add ¹/₂ cup cream, thyme, and remaining apples to soup and simmer for 5 minutes. In batches, purée soup in a blender (or use an immersion blender). Return to saucepan and season with salt and pepper. Serve hot in individual bowls, each serving garnished with a spoonful of reserved apples and drizzled with additional cream.

PORK CHOPS *with* CREAMY
CHANTERELLE SAUCE

WINE SUGGESTION: CALIFORNIA PINOT NOIR

Wild mushrooms pop up throughout the year when the weather conditions are right, but fall is the season for golden chanterelles. These trumpet-shaped fungi have an earthier flavor than their counterparts and are a perfect match for pork. Read more about varieties of mushrooms on page 129.

YOU WILL NEED

Four 8-ounce center-cut pork loin chops, cut 3/4 inch thick

Kosher salt and freshly ground black pepper

1/4 cup all-purpose flour

1 tablespoon vegetable oil

1 tablespoon unsalted butter

1 pound chanterelle mushrooms, rinsed well and sliced

2 tablespoons minced shallots

1/2 cup dry sherry

1 cup canned low-sodium chicken broth

1/2 teaspoon dried thyme

1/2 cup sour cream or plain yogurt

2 teaspoons cornstarch

1 Season chops with 1/2 teaspoon salt and 1/4 teaspoon pepper. Dredge in flour and shake off excess flour.

2 Heat oil over medium-high heat in a heavy 12-inch skillet. Add chops and cook, turning once, until browned on both sides, about 4 minutes. Transfer to a plate.

3 Add butter to skillet and melt. Add mushrooms and cook, stirring often, until they give off their juices and begin to brown, about 10 minutes. (Chanterelles can give off a lot of liquid during cooking. If liquid is excessive, pour it off during cooking to encourage browning.) Stir in shallots and cook until they soften, about 2 minutes. Add sherry and boil to reduce by half. Stir in broth and thyme. Return chops to skillet and reduce heat to medium-low. Cover tightly and cook until chops are cooked through, about 25 minutes. Transfer chops to a platter.

4 In a small bowl, whisk sour cream and cornstarch together to dissolve cornstarch. Whisk into cooking liquid and bring to a simmer to lightly thicken sauce. Season with salt and pepper. Pour over chops and serve at once.

PARMIGIANO TILAPIA

with **FENNEL & POTATOES**

MAIN COURSE

MAKES 4 SERVINGS

WINE SUGGESTION: CALIFORNIA SAUVIGNON BLANC

When eaten raw, fennel has a pronounced licorice flavor. However, roasted fennel has an entirely different sweet flavor that pairs beautifully with fish and potatoes. The addition of Parmigiano-Reggiano cheese ties the various elements together.

YOU WILL NEED

3 tablespoons extra-virgin olive oil

3 red-skinned potatoes (about 1 pound), halved lengthwise, then crosswise into ½-inch-thick half-moons

2 fennel bulbs (about 12 ounces each), trimmed (fronds reserved)

Kosher salt and freshly ground black pepper

Four 4-ounce tilapia fillets

½ cup (2 ounces) freshly grated Parmigiano-Reggiano

1 Preheat oven to 400°F.

2 Heat 2 tablespoons of oil in a very large ovenproof skillet over medium-high heat. Add potatoes and cook, stirring occasionally, until lightly browned, about 5 minutes.

3 Meanwhile, cut each fennel bulb in half lengthwise. Cut out and discard tough cores. Cut each half crosswise into ½-inch-thick slices. Add to skillet, drizzle with remaining 1 tablespoon oil, and season with 1 teaspoon salt and ½ teaspoon pepper. Toss well. Place skillet in oven and bake, stirring after 15 minutes, until potatoes and fennel are almost tender, about 30 minutes.

4 Season tilapia with ½ teaspoon salt and ¼ teaspoon pepper. Remove skillet from oven. Sprinkle potato mixture with ¼ cup of Parmigiano-Reggiano. Arrange tilapia over potato mixture and sprinkle fillets with remaining ¼ cup cheese. Return skillet to oven and bake until fish is opaque when flaked in the thickest part with the tip of a small, sharp knife, about 8 minutes.

5 Just before serving, finely chop enough reserved fennel fronds to make 1 tablespoon. Sprinkle over fish and serve hot.

CLASSIC ROAST TURKEY

MAIN COURSE

with **ROSEMARY GRAVY**

MAKES 16 SERVINGS

WINE SUGGESTION: OREGON PINOT NOIR

Millions of families serve turkey every Thanksgiving, but few know how to keep the white meat from drying out. Here's the secret: Wrap the breast with aluminum foil, which slows down the cooking and protects the lean meat from drying out. During the last hour of roasting, remove the foil, baste the bird a couple of times, and you will end up with a picture-perfect turkey.

YOU WILL NEED

One 20-pound turkey

Fall Vegetable Stuffing with Sausage (page 128)

$1/2$ cup (1 stick) unsalted butter, melted, plus more if needed

1 tablespoon kosher salt

1 teaspoon freshly ground black pepper

3 cups water

7 $1/2$ cups Quick Turkey Stock (page 119), or as needed

$3/4$ cup all-purpose flour

1 tablespoon plus 1 teaspoon minced fresh rosemary, or 2 teaspoons crumbled dried rosemary

1 Preheat oven to 325°F. Remove giblets and neck from turkey; reserve for Quick Turkey Stock. Discard liver or save for another use. Rinse turkey inside and out with cold water; pat dry with paper towels. Pull off pale yellow fat on both sides of tail and reserve.

2 Loosely fill neck cavity with some of stuffing; do not pack stuffing. Fold over neck skin and secure to back skin with a metal or bamboo skewer. Loosely fill body cavity with some of remaining stuffing. Cover exposed stuffing with a piece of foil. Place any remaining stuffing in a lightly buttered casserole, cover with lid or aluminum foil, and refrigerate to bake later as a side dish. Tie ends of drumsticks together with kitchen twine, or tuck them under flap of skin (or plastic or metal "hock lock"). Lift wing tips up and over back and tuck them under bird.

continued

3 Place turkey on a roasting rack set in a roasting pan. Add reserved turkey fat to pan. Generously brush turkey all over with $1/2$ cup melted butter and sprinkle inside and out with salt and pepper. Tightly cover breast area (not wings) with aluminum foil. Add water to pan. Bake, basting every 45 minutes or so (including area under foil) until an instant-read thermometer inserted in meaty part of thigh (not touching bone) registers 180°F, about 4 $3/4$ hours. During last hour of roasting, remove and discard foil. As water in roasting pan evaporates, add additional water to keep drippings from scorching.

4 Transfer turkey to a large serving platter, reserving pan drippings for gravy. Let turkey stand uncovered for at least 30 minutes before carving. Increase oven temperature to 350°F. Drizzle $1/2$ cup of turkey stock over stuffing in casserole, cover, and bake until heated through, about 30 minutes. (If you like crispy stuffing, remove foil after 15 minutes.)

5 Meanwhile, pour reserved pan drippings into a heatproof glass bowl or large measuring cup. Let stand for 5 minutes, then skim off and reserve clear yellow fat that has risen to top. Measure $3/4$ cup fat, adding melted butter (or better yet, solidified fat from Quick Turkey Stock on page 119), if needed. Add enough turkey stock to skimmed drippings to make 8 cups total.

6 Place roasting pan on two stove burners over medium-low heat and add reserved liquid turkey fat. Whisk in flour, scraping up browned bits on bottom of pan, and cook until flour is lightly browned, about 2 minutes. Whisk in turkey stock mixture and rosemary. Cook over medium heat, whisking often, until gravy has thickened and no trace of flour taste remains, about 5 minutes. Keep gravy warm until ready to serve.

7 Strain gravy through sieve into heatproof bowl, if desired. Pour into a warmed gravy boat. Carve turkey and serve gravy and stuffing alongside.

QUICK TURKEY STOCK

Heat 2 teaspoons vegetable oil in a large, heavy saucepan over medium-high heat. Chop turkey neck with a heavy knife or cleaver into 2-inch chunks. Add neck, heart, and gizzard to pot. Cook uncovered, turning occasionally, until turkey parts are browned, about 7 minutes. Add 1 chopped small yellow onion, 1 peeled and chopped small carrot, and 1 chopped small celery stalk with its leaves. Cook, stirring occasionally, until they soften, about 5 minutes.

Stir in 3 $\frac{1}{2}$ cups reduced-sodium chicken or vegetable broth and enough cold water to cover ingredients by 1 inch. Bring to a boil over high heat, skimming off any foam that rises to surface. Add 3 fresh flat-leaf parsley sprigs, $\frac{1}{2}$ teaspoon dried thyme, $\frac{1}{4}$ teaspoon black peppercorns, and 1 bay leaf. Reduce heat to low and simmer, uncovered, for at least 1 hour or up to 2 hours. Strain stock through a colander into a large heatproof bowl, discarding solids. Skim fat from surface of stock and reserve it for making gravy. Makes about 8 cups.

ESTIMATED TURKEY ROASTING TIMES

Use this chart to estimate the roasting time (at 325°F) for any size of turkey, stuffed or unstuffed. Extra time has been factored in to each weight category to allow for variations in roasting conditions, such as the temperature of the refrigerated bird.

UNSTUFFED TURKEY		STUFFED TURKEY	
8 to 12 pounds	2 $\frac{3}{4}$—3 hours	8 to 12 pounds	3—3 $\frac{1}{2}$ hours
12 to 14 pounds	3—3 $\frac{3}{4}$ hours	12 to 14 pounds	3 $\frac{1}{2}$—4 hours
14 to 18 pounds	3 $\frac{3}{4}$—4 $\frac{1}{4}$ hours	14 to 18 pounds	4—4 $\frac{1}{4}$ hours
18 to 20 pounds	4 $\frac{1}{4}$—4 $\frac{1}{2}$ hours	18 to 20 pounds	4 $\frac{1}{4}$—4 $\frac{3}{4}$ hours
20 to 24 pounds	4 $\frac{1}{2}$—5 hours	20 to 24 pounds	4 $\frac{3}{4}$—5 $\frac{1}{4}$ hours

TIPS FOR A PERFECT TURKEY

Don't underestimate how much turkey to buy. **To ensure** enough meat for leftovers and seconds, allow at least 1 pound of uncooked turkey for each person. Large tom turkeys (about 14 pounds and up) have more meat on their bones than do smaller hens, but this is a good rule of thumb.

Be flexible with roasting times. **There are many variables** that can affect the roasting time: the temperature of the turkey, inaccurate oven temperature, too-frequent opening of the oven door (which drops the temperature), and even the temperature of the stuffing. Tack an additional 30 minutes onto the estimated roasting time, just to be sure.

Use an accurate meat thermometer. **Use the pop-up** thermometer as an indicator that the turkey might be done, but back it up with a digital meat thermometer. Insert the thermometer in the thickest part of thigh (between the thigh and the drumstck), not touching the bone.

Stuff warm stuffing in a cold turkey. **Contrary to what** you might think, it is best to stuff a turkey with warm, freshly made stuffing. Stuffing must be cooked to 160°F to kill any potentially harmful bacteria, so it has a better chance of reaching that temperature if the stuffing is warm.

Let the turkey rest before carving. **A rest period before** carving (for the turkey, not the cook) is one of the secrets to a moist, juicy bird. The hot juices in the turkey must cool and relax back into the meat—if carved too soon, they will squirt out and contribute to dry meat. The larger the bird, the longer it can stand at room temperature without cooling off. Allow 30 minutes for an average-sized bird of about 15 pounds, and up to 1 hour for large birds around 20 pounds. With the turkey on the platter, the oven is now free for reheating side dishes.

CELERY ROOT & POTATO

PURÉE *with* GRUYÈRE

There is nothing wrong with traditional mashed potatoes—we'll happily eat them anytime. But try this variation the next time you make them, and you will probably hear "These are the best mashed potatoes I ever ate" from at least one guest. Celery root (also called celeriac) and Gruyère cheese are the secret ingredients.

YOU WILL NEED

1 large celery root (about 2 ½ pounds), peeled and cut into 2-inch chunks

2 large baking (russet) potatoes (about 1 pound), peeled and cut into 2-inch chunks

½ cup whole milk, heated

4 tablespoons unsalted butter, at room temperature

1 cup (4 ounces) shredded Gruyère cheese

Kosher salt and freshly ground white or black pepper

1 Put celery root and potatoes in a large pot and add enough lightly salted water to cover by 1 inch. Bring to a boil over high heat. Reduce heat to medium-low and simmer until vegetables are tender when pierced with tip of a small, sharp knife, about 20 minutes. Drain well.

2 Return celery root and potatoes to pot and cook over medium-low heat, stirring often, to evaporate excess moisture, about 2 minutes. Remove from heat. Add milk and butter. Using a hand-held electric mixer on high speed (or a hand masher), whip (or mash) the vegetables to the desired consistency. Stir in the Gruyère. Season with salt and pepper. Transfer to a serving bowl and serve hot.

ROASTED VEGETABLES

on CILANTRO COUSCOUS

PASTA

MAKES 4—6 SERVINGS

WINE SUGGESTION: MERLOT

There are quicker techniques for cooking vegetables, but roasting brings out their flavor like no other method. Also, the vegetables leave caramelized juices in the pan that can be utilized for a sauce. Here is a mélange of vegetables, seasoned in the Moroccan manner, for spooning onto a bed of couscous.

YOU WILL NEED

1/4 cup extra-virgin olive oil

2 garlic cloves, crushed

1 butternut squash (1 3/4 pounds), peeled, seeded, and cut into 1-inch cubes

2 large zucchini, trimed and cut into 3/4-inch-thick rounds

1 turnip, peeled and cut into 1-inch cubes

1 red bell pepper, seeded, deribbed, and cut into 1-inch squares

1 large unpeeled yellow onion, cut into sixths

1 teaspoon ground cumin

1/2 teaspoon ground coriander

1/2 teaspoon ground ginger

Kosher salt

1/4 teaspoon cayenne pepper

1/4 teaspoon freshly ground black pepper

4 cups water

2 tablespoons tomato paste

One 10-ounce box couscous (1 1/2 cups)

3 tablespoons minced fresh cilantro

1 Preheat oven to 400°F.

2 Heat oil and garlic in a small saucepan over low heat until tiny bubbles surround garlic, about 5 minutes. Remove from heat and let garlic infuse oil while preparing vegetables.

3 Combine squash, zucchini, turnip, bell pepper, and onion in a large roasting pan. Strain garlic oil over vegetables, discarding garlic. Toss vegetables in oil. Roast until vegetables are tender and lightly browned, about 1 hour. Combine cumin, coriander, ginger, $1/2$ teaspoon salt, cayenne, and black pepper. During last 5 minutes of roasting, sprinkle spice mixture over vegetables and mix well. Transfer vegetables to a medium bowl.

4 Place roasting pan over two burners on high heat and heat until pan sizzles. Add 2 cups water and tomato paste and bring to a boil, scraping up any browned bits in bottom of pan with a wooden spoon. Boil until liquid reduces to $1\,3/4$ cups, about 2 minutes. Pour over vegetables.

5 Meanwhile, bring remaining 2 cups water and $1/2$ teaspoon salt to a boil in a medium saucepan. Stir in couscous. Remove from heat, cover, and let stand until couscous is tender, about 5 minutes. Fluff couscous with a fork. Stir in cilantro.

6 Spoon couscous onto plates and top with vegetables. Serve hot.

FETTUCCINE *with* PANCETTA &
BRUSSELS SPROUTS

PASTA

MAKES 4—6 SERVINGS

WINE SUGGESTION: UN-OAKED CALIFORNIA CHARDONNAY

While the appeal of spaghetti and tomato sauce cannot be denied, other ways to dress pasta have become equally popular. You may not have considered Brussels sprouts fair game for your pasta, but give it a try and you are likely to be very pleasantly surprised. Read more about Brussels sprouts on page 126.

YOU WILL NEED

3 tablespoons extra-virgin olive oil

4 ounces pancetta or bacon, cut into ¼-inch dice

20 ounces Brussels sprouts, very thinly sliced (easy to do in a food processor with a slicing blade)

⅓ cup minced shallots

3 garlic cloves, minced

1 cup reduced-sodium chicken broth

Grated zest of 1 lemon

3 tablespoons fresh lemon juice

1 pound fettuccine

½ cup (2 ounces) freshly grated Parmigiano-Reggiano, plus more for serving

Kosher salt and freshly ground black pepper

1 Bring a large pot of salted water to a boil over high heat.

2 Heat 1 tablespoon of oil in a large skillet over medium heat. Add pancetta and cook, stirring often, until lightly browned, about 5 minutes. Using a slotted spoon, transfer pancetta to a plate.

3 Add Brussels sprouts to fat in skillet and cook, stirring often, until wilted, about 5 minutes. Stir in shallots and garlic and cook, stirring often, until sprouts are just tender, about 2 minutes more. Add broth and lemon zest and juice and bring to a boil. Cook until broth is reduced by half, about 5 minutes. Set aside.

4 Meanwhile, add fettuccine to boiling lightly salted water and cook according to package directions until al dente. Drain and return to cooking pot.

5 Add sprouts mixture, cooked pancetta, and ½ cup Parmigiano-Reggiano and drizzle with remaining 2 tablespoons oil. Toss well and season with salt and pepper. Serve hot, with extra cheese passed on side.

BRUSSELS SPROUTS

These small green orbs resemble tiny cabbages, and in fact, they belong to the same botanical family, along with broccoli, kale, and collard greens. They are popular in Belgium and probably originated there. The cool weather of the region is perfect for their growth, as they grow best at temperatures around 55°F, making them a good autumn crop. In the United States, the foggy coastal areas of central California provide most of the nation's crop.

Until recently, Brussels sprouts were usually boiled, frequently to a fare-thee-well that did nothing for their color, texture, or aroma. Now, they are more often roasted or sautéed to retain their vitamins and enhance their flavor, as a light caramelization sweetens their naturally earthy flavor.

PENNE WITH CAULIFLOWER

& SAGE

PASTA

MAKES 4—6 SERVINGS

WINE SUGGESTION: PINOT GRIGIO

Italian cooks are endlessly resourceful and can make pasta sauce out of just about anything. Cauliflower is one of the many ingredients used in Italy, and once you taste this dish, you'll know why.

YOU WILL NEED

4 ounces pancetta or bacon slices, cut into small cubes

2 tablespoons extra-virgin olive oil

One 2-pound cauliflower, cut into florets about 1 inch wide

2 garlic cloves, minced

One 14.5-ounce can diced tomatoes in juice

2 tablespoons minced fresh sage, plus more for garnish

Kosher salt

Red pepper flakes

1 pound penne or other tubular pasta

Freshly grated Parmigiano-Reggiano, for serving

1 Bring a large pot of lightly salted water to a boil over high heat.

2 Cook pancetta and oil together in a large skillet over medium-high heat, stirring occasionally, until pancetta is crisp and brown, about 5 minutes. Using a slotted spoon, transfer pancetta to paper towels to drain.

3 Add cauliflower to fat in skillet. Cook, uncovered, turning occasionally, until cauliflower is lightly browned, about 5 minutes. Add garlic and stir until fragrant, about 1 minute. Stir in tomatoes with their juice, cooked pancetta, and 2 tablespoons sage. Season with salt and pepper flakes and bring to a simmer. Reduce heat to low and cover. Simmer until cauliflower is barely tender, about 15 minutes.

4 Meanwhile, add penne to boiling water and cook according to package directions until al dente. Drain and return pasta to hot pot.

5 Add sauce to penne and mix well. Serve at once, garnishing each serving with a sprinkle of sage, and passing Parmigiano-Reggiano on side.

FALL VEGETABLE STUFFING

with SAUSAGE

SIDE DISH

MAKES ABOUT 8 CUPS*
*OR 12 SIDE-DISH SERVINGS

You probably already have a favorite turkey stuffing (or dressing), but here is an unusually satisfying one that combines root vegetables and sausage. To save time, roast the vegetables and cook the sausage the night before, cool, and refrigerate in self-sealing plastic bags. When ready to make the stuffing, reheat the vegetables and sausage together in a large skillet over medium heat, stirring often, until hot.

YOU WILL NEED

1 pound firm white sandwich bread, cut into $1/2$-inch cubes

3 large carrots, peeled and cut into $1/2$-inch-thick rounds

2 large parsnips, peeled and cut into $1/2$-inch-thick rounds

1 celery root (about 1 $1/4$ pounds), peeled and cut into $1/2$-inch cubes

1 large yellow onion, cut into 6 wedges (leave root end intact)

4 tablespoons olive oil

1 pound pork or turkey Italian sausage, casings removed

$1/4$ cup chopped fresh flat-leaf parsley

2 tablespoons chopped fresh sage

1 $1/2$ cups Quick Turkey Stock (page 119), or as needed

Kosher salt and freshly ground black pepper

1 One day before making stuffing, spread bread cubes on a large baking sheet and let stand overnight at room temperature to dry. (Or, bake bread cubes in a preheated 300°F oven, stirring occasionally, until dried but not toasted, about 30 minutes. Let cool.)

2 Preheat oven to 450°F. Mix carrots, parsnips, celery root, and onion in a large bowl. Drizzle with 3 tablespoons of oil and toss to coat. Spread in a large roasting pan. Roast, stirring occasionally, until tender and browned, about 40 minutes. Transfer to a large bowl.

3 Heat remaining 1 tablespoon oil in a large skillet over medium heat. Add sausage and cook, occasionally stirring and breaking sausage into bite-sized pieces, until it is cooked through, about 10 minutes. Transfer to bowl with vegetables.

4 Add dried bread cubes, parsley, and sage and gradually stir in stock just until evenly moistened but not soggy. Season with salt and pepper. Use at once to stuff a turkey. Spread remaining stuffing in a buttered baking dish, cover with aluminum foil, and refrigerate until ready to bake. Bake in a preheated 350°F oven until heated through, 30 to 40 minutes. For crisp stuffing, remove foil after 20 minutes.

MUSHROOMS

Unlike plants, most varieties of mushrooms do not need chlorophyll in order to grow. In fact, they don't even need soil, and have the ability to turn their growing medium, which includes decomposing leaf mulch and logs, into carbohydrates and then into mushroom tissue.

Most commercial mushrooms have been cultivated, with their spores inoculated into a growing medium. By far the most common variety is *Agaricus bisporus*, a group that encompasses white (button), portobello, and cremini mushrooms. Shiitake and oyster mushrooms are other popular cultivated varieties. However, when the weather cooperates with rainy, moist growing conditions, our wild mushroom purveyors bring us golden chanterelles and spongy-looking morels.

Some cooks advise against rinsing mushrooms and suggest brushing each one clean with a soft-bristled mushroom brush. Not only is this tedious, it is unnecessary. However, mushrooms, and wild mushrooms, in particular, can harbor grit and other material in their gills and other crevices, and need thorough washing. Add the mushrooms to a large bowl of cold water and quickly agitate them in the water to loosen any dirt. This should only take a few seconds, as you don't want them to soak. Lift the mushrooms out of the water and transfer to a colander to drain completely. Pat the mushrooms dry with paper towels before cooking.

CRANBERRY SAUCE

The simple addition of crystallized ginger takes good old cranberry sauce to another level. While they are in season, buy extra cranberries and freeze them to make this sauce at other times of the year. It is fantastic with grilled pork chops or baked ham.

YOU WILL NEED

3 cups (12 ounces) cranberries, rinsed

1 1/2 cups sugar

1/2 cup coarsely chopped crystallized ginger

1/2 cup water

1 In a medium nonaluminum saucepan, bring cranberries, sugar, ginger, and water to a boil over medium heat, stirring often to dissolve sugar. Reduce heat to medium-low. Simmer, uncovered, stirring often, until all berries have burst, about 5 minutes.

2 Transfer sauce to a medium bowl and let cool completely. (Sauce can be made up to 1 week ahead, cooled, covered, and refrigerated.) Serve at room temperature.

· CREAMY APPLE ·

CROSTATA

When you don't have the time to peel apples for a double-crusted apple pie, make this Italian-inspired beauty. It's a free-form apple tart (similar to the Cherry Galette on page 99), with a fragrant nutmeg custard. Both Golden Delicious and Honeycrisp apples are nicely flavored and hold their shape after cooking.

YOU WILL NEED

PASTRY DOUGH

1 cup unbleached all-purpose flour

2 tablespoons sugar

1/2 teaspoon fine sea salt

1/2 cup (1 stick) cold unsalted butter, cut into very thin slices

3 tablespoons ice water, or as needed

3 tablespoons sugar

3 Golden Delicious or Honeycrisp apples, peeled, cored, and cut into 1/4-inch-thick slices (see note, page 132)

1/4 cup heavy cream

1 large egg yolk

1/4 teaspoon vanilla extract

1/4 teaspoon freshly grated nutmeg

1 Position a rack in bottom third of oven and preheat oven to 400°F. Line a baking sheet with parchment paper.

2 To make dough: Pulse flour, sugar, and salt in a food processor to combine. Add butter and pulse until mixture resembles coarse cornmeal with some lentil-sized pieces. Transfer to a medium bowl. (Or, mix flour, sugar, and salt in a medium bowl. Using a pastry blender, cut in butter.) Gradually stir in enough of water until dough clumps together. Gather up the dough and press into a thick disk. Use now, or wrap dough in plastic wrap and refrigerate for at least 30 minutes or up to 1 day. (Let well-chilled dough stand at room temperature to soften slightly before rolling out.)

continued

3 Place dough on a lightly floured work surface and dust with flour. Roll dough into a 12-inch round about $1/8$ inch thick. Transfer to lined baking sheet. Sprinkle center of dough round with 1 tablespoon of sugar, leaving a $1\,1/2$-inch border. Arrange apple slices in two overlapping concentric circles on sugar, filling in center with smaller slices. Sprinkle with 1 tablespoon of sugar. Fold dough border over, loosely pleating dough as needed. Brush away any flour from dough.

4 Bake until dough looks set, about 15 minutes. Whisk cream, egg yolk, vanilla, nutmeg, and remaining 1 tablespoon sugar until combined. Slowly pour over apples, letting custard fill in spaces around slices (crust will keep custard from spilling out, but pour slowly and don't use all of custard if it threatens to overflow crust). Bake until custard is set and apples are tender when pierced with tip of a sharp knife, about 20 minutes more.

5 Let cool on baking sheet for 15 minutes, then slide crostata off parchment paper onto a large plate. Serve warm or cooled to room temperature.

NOTE: Peeling, coring, and slicing apples for pie and other dishes can be a time-consuming chore, but here's a faster way. The idea is to slice the four quadrants off the core of the apple. Start by peeling the apple. Stand the apple on the work surface. Using a large knife, cut off a thick slice from one side of the apple, stopping just short of the tough core. Turn the apple ninety degrees, and cut off another quadrant of the apple in the same manner. Repeat twice, and you will have four large, evenly shaped chunks of apple and the core. Discard the core, and slice the chunks into the required thickness.

DOUBLE-CRUST FIG TART

This luscious crostata (Italy's answer to the tart) was created as an upscale version of a stuffed fig cookie. You can use your favorite fig, from Black Mission to Brown Turkey. The filling is a good way to use very ripe figs that won't last another day.

YOU WILL NEED

DOUGH

1 ²/₃ cups unbleached all-purpose flour

¹/₂ cup confectioners' sugar

1 teaspoon baking powder

¹/₄ teaspoon fine sea salt

¹/₂ cup (1 stick) cold unsalted butter, thinly sliced

1 large egg yolk, beaten

2 tablespoons whole milk

1 teaspoon vanilla extract

FILLING

2 pounds (about 6 cups) ripe figs, thickly sliced

¹/₃ cup plus 1 tablespoon granulated sugar

Grated zest of 1 lemon

2 tablespoons fresh lemon juice

2 tablespoons seedless raspberry preserves

1 large egg yolk beaten with 1 tablespoon milk, for glaze

1 To make dough: Using a whisk, stir flour, confectioners' sugar, baking powder, and salt in a medium bowl. Using a pastry blender, cut in butter until mixture resembles coarse meal. In a small bowl, mix egg yolk, milk, and vanilla. Stir into flour mixture to make a soft dough.

2 Gather dough into a ball, divide dough into two pieces, one slightly larger than the other, and form into disks. Wrap each in plastic wrap and refrigerate for at least 1 hour or up to overnight. Let well-chilled dough stand at room temperature to slightly soften for 30 minutes before using.

3 To make filling: Combine figs, sugar, and lemon zest and juice in a medium saucepan and bring to a boil over medium heat, stirring often. The figs will give off juices as they heat. Cover and cook for 5 minutes. Uncover and cook until thick, about 15 minutes. Transfer to a bowl and let cool completely.

continued

4 Position a rack in center of oven and preheat oven to 350°F. Lightly butter a 9-inch tart pan with a removable bottom.

5 Crumble larger disk of dough into pan. Using your fingertips or a wooden tart tamper, press dough evenly into pan and up sides, making a sharp 90-degree angle where sides meet bottom of pan. Spread preserves over bottom of crust, then spread with cooled fig filling. Place remaining dough disk on a lightly floured work surface and sprinkle top with flour. Roll out into a 9 1/2-inch round. Roll dough onto rolling pin, then unroll it over fig filling. Press edges of top and bottom crusts together to seal. Roll rolling pin over top of pan to remove any excess dough. Cut a few slits in center of top crust in a decorative pattern. Lightly brush top crust with egg yolk mixture.

6 Place on a baking sheet and bake until crust is golden brown, about 45 minutes. Transfer to a wire rack and let cool for 10 minutes. Remove sides of tart pan and let tart cool completely on rack. Serve at room temperature.

AUTUMN PLUM CAKE

DESSERT

MAKES 12 SERVINGS

You can make this sweet treat whenever plums are in season, but it is an especially good way to use autumn's purple Italian prune plums, which are firmer and juicier than their counterparts. Serve with a glass of sweet wine.

YOU WILL NEED

1 1/3 cups unbleached all-purpose flour

1 1/2 teaspoons baking powder

1/4 teaspoon fine sea salt

1/2 cup plus 6 tablespoons (1 3/4 sticks) unsalted butter, at room temperature

1 cup plus 1 tablespoon granulated sugar

4 large eggs, at room temperature

1/2 teaspoon vanilla extract

12 ripe smallish Italian prune plums, halved lengthwise and pitted

1/4 teaspoon ground cinnamon

Confectioners' sugar, for dusting

1 Position a rack in center of oven and preheat oven to 350°F. Butter and flour a 9-by-13-inch baking pan and tap out excess flour.

2 Using a whisk, stir flour, baking powder, and salt together in a medium bowl. Beat butter and 1 cup of sugar together in a medium bowl with an electric mixer on high speed until mixture is light and fluffy, about 3 minutes. One at a time, beat in eggs, then vanilla. On low speed, add flour mixture in two additions and beat just until smooth, scraping down sides of bowl as needed. Spread evenly in pan. Arrange 4 rows of 6 plum halves, cut side up, on batter. Combine remaining 1 tablespoon sugar with cinnamon and sprinkle over plums.

3 Bake until a toothpick inserted in center of cake batter (not a plum) comes out clean, about 30 minutes. Let cool completely in pan on a wire rack.

4 To serve, sift confectioners' sugar over cake and cut into rectangles.

SWEET POTATO CAKE

with ORANGE ICING

Sweet potatoes make a moist cake that may remind you of carrot cake. Use the large holes on a box grater to shred them. One important tip: Nonstick fluted tube pans (also called Bundt pans) soak up oven heat because of their dark color, making the cake batter bake at a faster rate, so reduce the oven temperature by 25°F to compensate.

YOU WILL NEED

Softened butter and fine dried bread cumbs, for the pan

CAKE

2 1/2 cups unbleached all-purpose flour

1 tablespoon baking powder

1 teaspoon ground cinnamon

1 teaspoon freshly grated nutmeg

1/2 teaspoon fine sea salt

1 1/2 cups vegetable oil

2 cups granulated sugar

4 large eggs, at room temperature

Grated zest of 1 orange

1/4 cup fresh orange juice

1 1/2 cups peeled and shredded orange-fleshed sweet potatoes (yams), such as Louisiana or Jewel

One 20-ounce can crushed pineapple in juice, well drained

1 cup coarsely chopped pecans

1 cup golden or dark raisins

ICING

1 cup confectioners' sugar

1/4 cup fresh orange juice

2 tablespoons water, or as needed

1 To make cake, preheat oven to 350°F (325°F if using a dark pan). Lightly butter a 10-inch fluted tube pan (Bundt pan), even if it is nonstick. Coat inside of pan with dried bread crumbs and tap out the excess crumbs.

2 Sift flour, baking powder, cinnamon, nutmeg, and salt together into a bowl. Beat oil and sugar together in a large bowl with an electric mixer on high speed. One at a time, beat in eggs, then orange zest and orange juice. On low speed, add flour mixture in three additions, stopping to scrape down sides of bowl as necessary. Stir in sweet potatoes, pineapple, pecans, and raisins. Spread evenly in pan.

continued

3 Bake until cracks in surface of cake seem dry and cake is beginning to shrink from sides of pan, about 1 hour (about 1 $1/4$ hours if using a dark pan at 325°F). Transfer to a wire rack and let cool for 10 minutes. Invert and unmold cake onto rack and let cool completely.

4 To make icing, whisk confectioners' sugar, orange juice, and enough water as needed to make an icing with consistency of heavy cream.

5 Place cake on rack on a rimmed baking sheet. Slowly pour icing over top of cake to coat as evenly as possible, letting icing run down sides of cake. Let icing stand until firm, about 1 hour. (Cake can be made 1 day ahead, wrapped in plastic wrap, and stored at room temperature.)

PUMPKIN JUMBLES

These may well be the perfect autumn cookie, moist and cakey with pumpkin, spices, dried cranberries, and walnuts, with an old-fashioned goodness that is comforting on a cold day. If you have a sweet tooth, the icing is a nice touch, but is entirely optional.

YOU WILL NEED

COOKIES

2 cups unbleached all-purpose flour

1 teaspoon baking soda

¹/₂ teaspoon ground cinnamon

¹/₂ teaspoon ground allspice

¹/₂ teaspoon ground nutmeg

¹/₄ teaspoon fine sea salt

¹/₂ cup (1 stick) unsalted butter, at room temperature

1 cup granulated sugar

1 cup canned pumpkin

1 large egg, beaten, at room temperature

1 cup chopped walnuts

1 cup dried cranberries

ICING

4 tablespoons unsalted butter

¹/₂ cup packed light brown sugar, rubbed through a sieve

4 tablespoons whole milk, or as needed

1 cup confectioners' sugar, or as needed

¹/₃ cup chopped walnuts

1 Position oven racks in top third and center of oven and preheat oven to 375°F. Line two baking sheets with parchment paper.

2 To make cookies: Sift flour, baking soda, cinnamon, allspice, nutmeg, and salt together. Beat butter and granulated sugar together in a medium bowl with an electric mixer on medium speed just until light and fluffy, about 2 minutes. Beat in pumpkin. Increase mixer speed to high and gradually beat in egg; mixture may curdle, but will smooth out after about 20 seconds of beating. With mixer on low, gradually beat in flour mixture, scraping down sides of bowl as needed. Mix in walnuts and cranberries.

continued

3 Drop dough by rounded tablespoonfuls about 2 inches apart onto lined baking sheets. Bake, switching baking sheets from top to bottom and front to back halfway through baking, until cookies are lightly browned and can be lifted easily from baking sheets, 12 to 15 minutes. Let cool on baking sheets for 5 minutes. Transfer cookies to wire racks to cool completely.

4 To make icing: Melt butter in a medium saucepan over medium-low heat. Add brown sugar and whisk until mixture is smooth and melted. Simmer for 2 minutes. Add 2 tablespoons milk and whisk well. Remove from heat and let cool until warm, about 15 minutes. Add confectioners' sugar. Whisk in enough of remaining milk to make an icing about consistency of heavy cream. Holding each cookie upside down, dip into icing to coat and wipe off excess icing with a small metal spatula. Transfer to wire rack and sprinkle with chopped walnuts. Let stand until icing sets. (Cookies can be stored in an airtight container for up to 5 days.)

BUILDER

APPETIZER
Smoked Salmon & Herb Tartlets 147

SOUP & SALADS
Oyster & Leek Chowder 149

DF GF V I Romaine Hearts with Avocado, Grapefruit & Red Onion 151

DF GF V I Kale & Quinoa Salad 153

MAIN COURSES
DF GF Chicken Breasts with Lemon, Garlic & Rosemary 155

Rack of Lamb with Pistachio Crust & Pomegranate Sauce 157

Oven-Barbecued Country Ribs 159

Jambalaya the Big Easy Way 160

DF GF Garlic-Herb Standing Rib Roast 163

GF Short Ribs Provençale 164

DF GF Beef Tenderloin with Shiraz Marinade 167

GF Pork Tenderloin with Parsnip-Bacon Hash 169

I Portobello Croque-Monsieur 171

PASTAS, RISOTTO & SIDE DISHES
GF Sausage & Radicchio Risotto 173

Fettuccine with Shrimp & Creamy Lemon Sauce 175

I Three-Cheese Macaroni & Cheese 177

GF I Roasted Fingerling Potatoes with Crème Fraîche & Herbs 179

V I Potato & Carrot Pancakes 180

GF I Mashed Turnips with Garlic 182

DESSERTS
I Chocolate-Banana Cream Pie 183

I Poached Pears in Spiced Port Syrup 187

DF DAIRY-FREE　**GF** GLUTEN-FREE　**V** VEGAN　**I** VEGETARIAN

WINTER

WINTER CAN HOLD MANY PLEASURES

FOR THE COOK WHO WANTS TO PREPARE MEALS WITH FRESH AND LOCAL PRODUCE.

Hearty greens, such as kale and radicchio, replace their more delicate cousins. Potatoes dug while the soil was still workable are now prepared in countless ways. An array of citrus fruits—oranges, tangerines, lemons, and grapefruits—bring bright colors and flavors to the table in dishes both savory and sweet. This is the season for simmering up a satisfying stew, or cooking a large roast for a big holiday celebration.

WINE SUGGESTION: CHAMPAGNE

When the winter round of parties arrives, it is good to have a reliable make-ahead appetizer to serve with drinks. These individual tartlets of cream cheese topped with lush smoked salmon fill the bill. You will need two 12-cup mini muffin pans. A wooden tart tamper will make the job of pressing the dough into the pans a very simple chore.

YOU WILL NEED

DOUGH

1 cup unbleached all-purpose flour

Pinch of fine sea salt

7 tablespoons unsalted butter, cut into 1/4-inch cubes, at room temperature

One 3-ounce package cream cheese, at room temperature

FILLING

One 8-ounce package cream cheese, at room temperature

1 large egg

1 large egg yolk

1/4 teaspoon kosher salt

1/8 teaspoon red pepper sauce

———

3 ounces sliced smoked salmon, coarsely chopped (about 1/2 cup)

Minced fresh dill or chives, for serving

1 To make dough: Pulse flour and salt together in a food processor. Add butter and cream cheese and pulse about 10 times, or until dough is crumbly. (Or, cream butter, cream cheese, and salt together in a medium bowl with an electric hand mixer on high speed, just until combined. With mixer on low speed, gradually beat in flour until dough clumps together.) Gather dough into a thick disk, wrap in plastic wrap, and refrigerate until chilled and firm, at least 2 hours or up to 1 day.

2 Preheat oven to 350°F. Have ready two 12-cup mini muffin pans. If pans are not nonstick, lightly butter cups.

continued

3 On a lightly floured work surface, divide dough into 24 pieces and roll each into a ball. Place a dough ball in a muffin cup and press it firmly with wooden tart tamper or your fingertips to evenly cover bottom and sides of muffin cup. Freeze pans for 5 minutes to firm dough.

4 To make filling: With an electric mixer on low speed (or with a wooden spoon) beat cream cheese, egg, egg yolk, salt, and red pepper sauce together in a small bowl until smooth. Spoon filling evenly into pastry shells.

5 Bake until shells are golden brown and filling is puffed, about 25 minutes. Let cool in pans for 5 minutes. Run a dinner knife around edge of each pastry shell to loosen, then remove tartlets from pans. Let cool completely on wire racks. (Tartlets can be baked up to 8 hours ahead, covered loosely, and refrigerated.)

6 Top each tartlet with a piece of smoked salmon and a sprinkle of dill. Serve at once.

OYSTER & LEEK CHOWDER

SOUP

MAKES 6—8 SERVINGS

WINE SUGGESTION: CHARDONNAY

Oysters are at their plumpest and juiciest in the winter, as they grow best in cold water. Consider this rich soup when you need a special first course for a holiday dinner, but serve it in small cups so guests don't fill up before the entrée.

YOU WILL NEED

1 large baking (russet) potato, peeled and cut into 3/4-inch cubes

4 bacon slices, coarsely chopped

3 tablespoons unsalted butter

2 large leeks, white and pale green parts only, chopped and well rinsed (1 1/2 cups)

2 large celery stalks, cut into 1/2-inch dice

3 tablespoons all-purpose flour

4 1/2 cups whole milk

1 pint shucked oysters, drained, juices reserved (cut large oysters in half)

Kosher salt and freshly ground black pepper

Minced fresh flat-leaf parsley, for serving

1 Put potato in a medium saucepan and add cold salted water to cover by 1 inch. Bring to a boil over high heat. Reduce heat to medium-low and simmer until tender when pierced with tip of a sharp knife, about 20 minutes. Drain potatoes.

2 In a large, heavy saucepan, cook bacon over medium heat, stirring occasionally, until crisp and browned, about 10 minutes. Using a slotted spoon, transfer bacon to paper towels to drain. Discard bacon fat, or save for another use.

3 Add butter to saucepan and melt over medium-low heat. Add leeks and celery and cover. Cook, stirring occasionally, until leeks are tender, about 5 minutes. Sprinkle with flour, stir well, and let cook without browning for 1 minute.

4 Stir in milk and drained oyster juices and bring to a boil over medium heat. Reduce heat to medium-low and simmer, stirring often, for 5 minutes to blend flavors. Add oysters, potatoes, and bacon and simmer just until oysters are plump and the edges curl, about 1 minute. Season with salt and pepper. Ladle into bowls, sprinkle with parsley, and serve hot.

ROMAINE HEARTS

SALAD

DF | GF | ⅄ | ▯

with **AVOCADO, GRAPEFRUIT & RED ONION**

MAKES 4 SERVINGS

This crisp salad has a mildly sweet dressing that accents the grapefruit. The avocados (tossed with a couple of tablespoons of the dressing), the soaked and drained onions, and the grapefruit sections can be prepared up to 8 hours ahead, stored in individual self-sealing plastic bags, and refrigerated. When it comes time to serve, it will take only a few minutes to toss it all together, especially because packaged romaine hearts usually do not need to be rinsed and dried. If you use conventional romaine lettuce, it can be cleaned, wrapped in paper towels, and refrigerated in a large plastic bag for up to 8 hours.

YOU WILL NEED

DRESSING

1/4 cup red wine vinegar

2 tablespoons honey

1/2 teaspoon salt

1/2 teaspoon freshly ground black pepper

3/4 cup vegetable oil

1 red onion, halved lengthwise and thinly sliced into half-moons

One 18-ounce package romaine lettuce hearts, torn into bite-sized pieces

2 large grapefruits, peeled and segmented

3 ripe avocados, pitted, peeled, and cut into 3/4-inch cubes

1 To make dressing: In a blender, combine vinegar, honey, salt, and pepper. With machine running, gradually add oil to make a thick dressing.

2 Soak onion in a bowl of cold water for 30 minutes to soften its sharpness. Drain well and pat dry with paper towels.

3 Just before serving, combine lettuce, grapefruits, avocados, and onion in a large serving bowl. Add dressing and toss to coat. Serve at once.

KALE & QUINOA SALAD

SALAD

DF | GF | Y | V

MAKES 4 SERVINGS

This healthful recipe uses kale as a salad green and combines it with nutty quinoa and sweet apples. You can use either curly or dark green Tuscan kale here. Serve this dish as a light lunch, as a side dish with grilled chicken, or as a main-course salad with the addition of leftover holiday turkey.

YOU WILL NEED

$^3/_4$ cup quinoa

1 $^1/_2$ cups water

Kosher salt

8 ounces kale, tough stems removed, washed well, dried, and cut crosswise into $^1/_2$-inch strips

2 tablespoons fresh lemon juice

2 unpeeled sweet apples, such as Honeycrisp or Gala, cored and coarsely chopped

$^1/_2$ cup coarsely chopped pecans

$^1/_2$ cup dried cranberries

3 tablespoons extra-virgin olive oil

Freshly ground black pepper

1 Put quinoa in a fine-mesh sieve and rinse well under cold running water. Combine quinoa, water, and $^1/_4$ teaspoon salt in medium saucepan and bring to a boil over high heat. Reduce heat to low and cover. Simmer until quinoa is tender and liquid is almost absorbed, 15 to 20 minutes. Drain in sieve and rinse under cold running water to cool quinoa. Press excess liquid from quinoa with back of a large spoon.

2 Combine kale, lemon juice, and $^1/_2$ teaspoon salt in a large bowl. Using your hands, rub ingredients together well until kale is wilted, 1 to 2 minutes. Fluff quinoa with a fork. Add quinoa to the kale with apples, pecans, and cranberries. Drizzle with oil and toss well. Season with salt and pepper. Serve at once. (Salad can be refrigerated for up to 1 day.)

KALE & COLLARD GREENS

Cabbage and its cousins, all members of the Cruciferae (formerly known as Brassicaceae) family, have long been invaluable food sources in cold climates; cabbage because it can be harvested and then stored for a long time, and cruciferous greens because they can be grown even when snow is on the ground.

Curly kale, dark green Tuscan kale (also known as lacinato or dinosaur kale), and smooth-leafed collard greens are closely related to cabbage, although they grow in a leafy manner instead of a ball, and the leaves can be cut from the ground as needed. The traditional method of cooking greens with pork turned out to be a beneficial one, as the vitamins in both kale and collards are fat-soluble, and added fat allows the body to absorb the nutrients. The common way to cook these greens is by long simmering, the better to calm their inherent bitterness. To this day, if you get greens at a barbecue restaurant, they have probably been made in this time-honored manner. However, our collective palate now appreciates stronger flavors, and many cooks stir-fry the greens just until they are crisp-tender, or even serve them raw in salads. If you are serving them uncooked, a rub with salt and lemon juice breaks down the cellulose and makes the greens more tender.

These bitter greens grow close to the ground and must be washed well to remove any dirt. To prepare them, soak in a sink of cold water for a few minutes, moving the leaves around in the water to loosen any grit. Lift out the leaves, leaving the dirt at the bottom of the sink. Tear out the tough central stem from each leaf. The leaves are now ready for chopping. For salads and stir-fries, dry the leaves, but for most other recipes, leave the water clinging to the leaves to provide moisture during cooking.

CHICKEN BREASTS

MAIN COURSE

DF | GF | 🍷

MAKES 4 SERVINGS

with **LEMON, GARLIC & ROSEMARY**

WINE SUGGESTION: PINOT GRIGIO

Lemon chicken is a staple of the Italian-American kitchen, and there are innumerable versions. Some are made in a skillet, a few are roasted. For crisp poultry skin and a brown, lemon-tart sauce, combine the methods for optimum results. Use vegetable broth to make this recipe gluten-free.

YOU WILL NEED

3 large lemons

1 tablespoon extra-virgin olive oil

Four 12-ounce bone-in, skin-on chicken breast halves

Kosher salt and freshly ground black pepper

$1/2$ cup reduced-sodium chicken or vegetable broth

1 teaspoon cornstarch

1 garlic clove, minced

2 teaspoons minced fresh rosemary, plus more for garnish

1 Preheat oven to 400°F. Slice 1 lemon into $1/4$-inch-thick rounds. Grate zest from 1 lemon. Squeeze juice from 2 whole lemons; you should have $1/3$ cup.

2 Heat oil in a large ovenproof skillet over medium-high heat. Season chicken with 1 teaspoon salt and $1/2$ teaspoon pepper. In batches, add chicken to oil, skin side down. Cook until skin is well browned, about 4 minutes. Transfer to a platter.

3 Pour off all but 2 tablespoons of fat from pan. Return chicken to pan, skin side up, and top with lemon slices. Transfer skillet to oven. Bake, basting occasionally with juices in skillet, until an instant-read thermometer inserted in thickest part of chicken registers 165°F, about 35 minutes. Transfer chicken with lemon slices to a deep serving platter.

4 Let skillet cool slightly. Mix lemon juice and broth in a small bowl. Sprinkle cornstarch over liquids and whisk to dissolve. Add garlic to fat in pan and stir over medium heat until fragrant, about 30 seconds. Whisk in lemon mixture, 2 teaspoons rosemary, and lemon zest. Bring to a boil, whisking to scrape up browned bits in pan, and cook until sauce is lightly thickened, about 30 seconds. Season with salt and pepper. Pour sauce over chicken, sprinkle with additional rosemary, and serve at once.

RACK OF LAMB

with **PISTACHIO CRUST & POMEGRANATE SAUCE**

WINE SUGGESTION: OREGON PINOT NOIR

Roast rack of lamb makes an impressive showing as a dinner party entrée for your very best friends. The colorful and tasty green pistachio crust, paired with a magenta-colored sauce, makes this dish even more special and provides colors of the season. You may think that you'll need more sauce, but you won't—it is rich.

YOU WILL NEED

2 racks of lamb (about 1 pound, 2 ounces each), frenched and trimmed of excess fat

2 tablespoons extra-virgin olive oil

1 ½ teaspoons minced fresh rosemary

Kosher salt and freshly ground black pepper

4 teaspoons Dijon mustard

1 garlic clove, crushed through a press

⅓ cup finely chopped pistachios

3 tablespoons panko (Japanese bread crumbs)

½ cup hearty red wine, such as Shiraz

½ cup reduced-sodium beef broth

½ cup bottled pomegranate juice

1 tablespoon cold unsalted butter

½ cup fresh pomegranate seeds, for garnish (see page 158)

1 Preheat oven to 400°F.

2 Brush lamb all over with 1 tablespoon of oil. Sprinkle with rosemary and season with 1 teaspoon salt and ½ teaspoon pepper. In a very large ovenproof skillet, heat remaining 1 tablespoon oil over medium-high heat. Add one rack of lamb, meaty side down, and cook until browned, about 3 minutes. Transfer to a plate and repeat with second rack of lamb. Pour out fat in skillet.

3 In a small bowl, mix mustard and garlic. Spread mustard mixture on meaty side of each rack. Combine pistachios and panko on a plate. Dip mustard-coated side of each rack in pistachio mixture and press to adhere. Stand racks, bones up, in skillet, intertwining bones.

continued

4 Bake until an instant-read thermometer inserted in center of a rack registers 130°F for medium-rare, 15 to 20 minutes. Transfer racks to a carving board and let stand for 5 to 10 minutes before carving.

5 Meanwhile, make sauce: Pour off all of fat and any crust crumbs from skillet, leaving browned bits in pan. Place skillet over high heat. Add wine, broth, and pomegranate juice and bring to a boil, scraping up browned bits in skillet with a wooden spoon. Boil until reduced to about $1/3$ cup, about 5 minutes. Remove from heat, add butter, and whisk until butter melts and lightly thickens sauce. Season with salt and pepper.

6 Cut each rack between bones to make 16 chops. Arrange 4 chops on each dinner plate, drizzle with about 1 tablespoon of sauce, and scatter with 2 tablespoons of pomegranate seeds. Serve hot.

NOTE: There is an easy way to remove pomegranate seeds from the white membrane. Using a sharp knife, score the pomegranate skin just down to the seeds. Place a large bowl in the sink and fill it with cold water. Submerge the pomegranate under the water and break it apart at the score marks. Using your fingers, work the seeds away from the membranes; they will sink and the membrane will float. Skim the membranes from the water. Drain the pomegranate seeds, transfer to an airtight container, and refrigerate for up to 3 days.

OVEN-BARBECUED
· COUNTRY RIBS ·

MAIN COURSE
MAKES 8 SERVINGS

WINE SUGGESTION: ZINFANDEL

Juicy ribs served hot off the grill are a warm-weather treat. When it's cold outside, here's how we make mouthwatering ribs in the oven. Meaty country ribs in a piquant sauce will fill your kitchen with appetizing aromas. See page 192 for suggestions on how to enjoy a gluten-free version of this recipe.

YOU WILL NEED

5 pounds bone-in country-style pork spareribs, cut into individual ribs

2 teaspoons kosher salt

1 teaspoon freshly ground black pepper

SAUCE

1 cup ketchup

3/4 cup water

1 yellow onion, finely chopped

1/2 cup fresh lemon juice

4 tablespoons unsalted butter

1 tablespoon Worcestershire sauce

1 tablespoon sweet Hungarian paprika or mild smoked paprika (pimentón)

2 teaspoons sugar

1 Position racks in center and upper third of oven and preheat oven to 350°F.

2 Season ribs with salt and pepper. Wrap 2 or 3 ribs securely in aluminum foil and repeat to make as many packets as needed. Place foil-wrapped ribs on baking sheets (they can overlap). Bake until ribs are almost tender (carefully open a foil packet to check), 1 1/2 to 2 hours.

3 Meanwhile, make sauce: Combine ketchup, water, onion, lemon juice, butter, Worcestershire, paprika, and sugar in a small, heavy saucepan. Bring to a boil over medium-high heat, stirring frequently. Let boil for 1 minute, then remove from heat.

4 Carefully unwrap each packet of ribs while they are still on the baking sheets and slather each batch with sauce. Reseal packets. Bake until ribs are fork-tender, about 1 hour more. Transfer rib packets to a cutting board and let stand for a few minutes. Carefully remove foil. Transfer ribs to a serving platter and serve hot.

· JAMBALAYA ·

THE BIG EASY WAY

MAIN COURSE

MAKES 6—8 SERVINGS

BEER SUGGESTION: LOUISIANA BEER, SUCH AS ABITA

Even if you can't be in New Orleans for Mardi Gras, you can cook the Cajun classic to celebrate the approach of the Easter season and spring. Warming and filling, jambalaya is a great winter dish, holiday or not. Converted rice, which has been par-cooked to remove excess starch, makes the best jambalaya because the grains cook up light and fluffy. See page 192 for suggestions on how to enjoy a gluten-free version of this recipe.

YOU WILL NEED

SEASONING

1 teaspoon kosher salt

1 teaspoon freshly ground black pepper

1 teaspoon freshly ground white pepper

1 teaspoon gumbo filé powder

1 teaspoon dry mustard

1 teaspoon dried thyme

1/2 teaspoon ground cumin

1/2 teaspoon cayenne pepper

——

5 tablespoons unsalted butter

6 ounces smoked ham, cut into bite-sized pieces

6 ounces andouille or kielbasa sausage, cut into bite-sized pieces

6 ounces sweet Italian sausage, casings removed

2 large yellow onions, chopped

4 celery stalks, chopped

1 green bell pepper, seeded, deribbed, and chopped

1 red bell pepper, seeded, deribbed, and chopped

4 garlic cloves, minced

5 bay leaves

3 cups converted white rice

6 cups reduced-sodium chicken broth

One 14.5-ounce can diced tomatoes in juice

1 pound large (21 to 25 count) shrimp, peeled, deveined, and butterflied

1 To make seasoning: Combine all seasoning ingredients in a small bowl.

2 In a Dutch oven or large, heavy saucepan, melt butter over medium-high heat. Add ham, andouille, and Italian sausage and cook, stirring occasionally with a wooden spoon and breaking up sausage with side of spoon, until Italian sausage loses its raw look, about 5 minutes.

3 Add onions, celery, bell peppers, garlic, and bay leaves and cook, stirring frequently and scraping up any browned bits from bottom of pot, until vegetables are softened and lightly browned at the edges, 8 to 10 minutes. Add seasoning and stir well.

4 Stir in rice and cook, stirring often to keep it from sticking to bottom of Dutch oven, until it turns opaque, about 5 minutes. Stir in broth and diced tomatoes with their juice and bring to a boil. Reduce heat to medium-low and cover. Simmer until rice is tender and liquid is absorbed, about 20 minutes.

5 During the last 5 minutes, add shrimp. Remove from heat and let stand for 5 minutes. Discard bay leaves and serve hot.

STANDING RIB ROAST

MAIN COURSE

DF | GF | 🍷

MAKES 8–10 SERVINGS

WINE SUGGESTION: CABERNET SAUVIGNON

A gorgeous rib roast, standing tall and proud, is reserved for special meals. Present the carved roast at the table, then high-tail it back into the kitchen for the actual slicing. As with all roasts, there are many variables (such as temperature of meat when it goes into the oven, and your oven's accuracy), so be flexible with your cooking times and let an instant-read thermometer be your guide to doneness. Use vegetable broth to make this recipe gluten-free.

YOU WILL NEED

One 8-pound bone-in standing rib beef roast (4 ribs), trimmed and tied

Extra-virgin olive oil

1 tablespoon kosher salt

6 garlic cloves, minced

1 tablespoon freshly ground black pepper

2 cups reduced-sodium beef or vegetable broth

2 teaspoons minced fresh thyme

---

1 Brush rib roast with oil. Season with salt. Combine garlic and pepper in a small bowl. Spread over roast. Loosely cover roast with plastic wrap and let stand at room temperature for 1 hour. Preheat oven to 350°F.

2 Place meat, bone side down, on a rack in a heavy roasting pan. Roast until an instant-read thermometer inserted in center of the roast registers 130°F for medium-rare, about 2 1/4 hours. Transfer roast to a carving board, tent with aluminum foil, and let stand for 20 minutes before carving.

3 Meanwhile, to make jus: Skim off and discard fat that has risen to top of pan juices. Heat roasting pan over medium heat. Add broth and thyme and bring to a boil over high heat, scraping up browned bits in the pan with a wooden spoon. Reduce heat to low and simmer for 5 minutes. Keep jus warm over low heat.

4 To carve roast, lay it on its side on a carving board. Using a carving fork to stabilize meat, run a sharp carving knife along rib bones, separating roast from ribs. Stand roast, cut side up, on carving board, and cut roast into 1/2-inch-thick slices. Cut between rib bones to separate them. Transfer sliced roast and ribs to a serving platter. Pour jus into a sauceboat. Serve beef au jus.

SHORT RIBS PROVENÇALE

MAIN COURSE

MAKES 6 SERVINGS

WINE SUGGESTION: ZINFANDEL OR SHIRAZ

Short ribs were once a cut that was cooked only when the budget was low. Now rediscovered and appreciated for their meaty texture and super-beefy flavor, they are at their best when slowly simmered to tenderness. Search out the meatiest short ribs, cut into individual pieces that weigh 12 to 16 ounces each. Serve the ribs and sauce the French way, spooned over buttered pasta.

YOU WILL NEED

2 tablespoons extra-virgin olive oil

6 pounds individual short ribs (not cross-cut flanken)

Kosher salt and freshly ground black pepper

1 large yellow onion, finely chopped

1 carrot, peeled and finely chopped

1 celery stalk, finely chopped

12 garlic cloves, crushed and peeled

2 tablespoons all-purpose flour

1 tablespoon herbes de Provençe

2 cups hearty red wine such as Zinfandel or Shiraz

1 3/4 cups reduced-sodium beef broth

One 14.5-ounce can diced tomatoes in juice, drained

1 bay leaf

8 ounces baby carrots

1/2 cup pitted Kalamata olives

3 tablespoons chopped fresh flat-leaf parsley, for garnish

1 Preheat oven to 300°F.

2 Heat oil in a very large Dutch oven or saucepan over medium-high heat. Season short ribs with 3/4 teaspoon salt and 1/2 teaspoon pepper. In batches, without crowding, add short ribs to pot and cook, turning occasionally, until browned on all sides, about 8 minutes. Transfer ribs to a platter.

3 Pour off all but 2 tablespoons of fat from Dutch oven. Add onion, carrot, and celery and reduce heat to medium-low. Cover and cook, stirring often, until vegetables have softened, about 5 minutes. Add garlic, flour, and herbes de Provençe and stir with a wooden spoon until garlic is fragrant, about 1 minute. Stir in wine and bring to a boil over high heat, stirring up any browned bits from bottom of pan. Add broth, tomatoes, and bay leaf. Return short ribs and any juices to pot. Add cold water as needed to barely reach top ribs and bring to a boil over high heat.

4 Cover tightly, transfer to oven, and bake, stirring occasionally to change position of ribs so they cook evenly, until meat is very tender, about 2 $1/2$ hours. During last 15 minutes, add baby carrots.

5 Transfer short ribs to a large, deep serving bowl and cover with aluminum foil to keep warm. Skim off fat from surface of cooking liquid and discard bay leaf. Bring to a boil over high heat and cook until liquid is reduced to a sauce consistency, about 10 minutes (exact time depends on size of pot). Add olives and cook to heat them through, about 3 minutes. Season sauce with salt and pepper.

6 Spoon sauce with carrots over ribs, sprinkle with parsley, and serve hot.

BEEF TENDERLOIN

with **SHIRAZ MARINADE**

MAIN COURSE

DF | GF | 🍷

MAKES 8 SERVINGS

WINE SUGGESTION: AUSTRALIAN CABERNET-SHIRAZ BLEND

There are many reasons to love beef tenderloin. It is tender, easy to carve, quick-cooking, and has a mild flavor that benefits from a rich marinade. No wonder it graces many a holiday table. While you can serve tenderloin with a sauce, offering it without one means it is easier to eat and dripless, a plus at buffets. This recipe calls for whole beef tenderloin, but you can use a trimmed roast, too, with delicious results. Use tamari sauce in the marinade to make this recipe gluten-free.

YOU WILL NEED

MARINADE

2 cups Australian Shiraz or other hearty dry red wine

$^1/_2$ cup extra-virgin olive oil

$^1/_4$ cup balsamic vinegar

$^1/_4$ cup soy sauce or tamari sauce

2 garlic cloves, minced

1 $^1/_2$ teaspoons dried basil

1 $^1/_2$ teaspoons dried rosemary

1 teaspoon kosher salt

$^1/_2$ teaspoon red pepper flakes

———

One 6-pound whole beef tenderloin, trimmed and tied (3 $^1/_2$) pounds trimmed weight; see note, page 168)

1 tablespoon extra-virgin olive oil for brushing

1 To make marinade: Whisk together all marinade ingredients in a large bowl, being sure to dissolve salt. Put tenderloin in a large glass or ceramic baking dish or a jumbo-sized self-sealing plastic storage bag. Pour in marinade and cover with plastic wrap (or close bag). Refrigerate, occasionally turning tenderloin in marinade, for at least 8 or up to 24 hours. Drain tenderloin and pat it dry with paper towels. Let stand at room temperature for 1 hour.

2 Preheat oven to 450°F. Lightly oil a large roasting pan.

continued

3 Brush tenderloin all over with oil. Place tenderloin in roasting pan. Roast for 10 minutes. Turn tenderloin and reduce heat to 350°F. Continue roasting until an instant-read thermometer inserted in center of meat registers 130°F, 20 to 30 minutes for medium-rare. Transfer to a carving board and let stand for 10 minutes.

4 Discard twine. Using a carving knife, cut tenderloin crosswise into $^1\!/_2$-inch-thick slices. Serve warm or cooled to room temperature.

HOME-TRIMMED TENDERLOIN: We offer trimmed and tied beef tenderloin at The Fresh Market. If you prefer to purchase a whole tenderloin and trim it at home, here's how to do it.

To trim tenderloin: Drain beef from its vacuum packaging and rinse under cold running water. (Any odor will dissipate in a minute or so.) Pat dry with paper towels. Using a sharp, thin-bladed knife, trim away any fat, including large lump at wide end, and discard. Pull and cut away long, thin "chain" muscle that runs length of tenderloin. Trim away fat from chain and reserve meat for another use. Following natural muscle separation, cut away large clod of meat at the wide end and reserve for another use. At one end of tenderloin, make an incision under silver sinew. Slip knife under sinew and pull and trim it away. Work lengthwise down tenderloin until it is completely free of sinew and fat. The trimmings will yield extra meat for a sauté or kebabs.

To tie home-trimmed tenderloin: Fold thin ends of tenderloin underneath bulk of meat so tenderloin is same thickness throughout its length, and tie in place with kitchen twine. Tie entire tenderloin crosswise at 2- to 3-inch intervals.

PORK TENDERLOIN

with **PARSNIP-BACON HASH**

MAKES 4—6 SERVINGS

WINE SUGGESTION: CALIFORNIA PINOT NOIR

Pork tenderloin roasts quickly, and while it is in the oven, you can create a tasty side dish of parsnips, apples, and bacon. Or, make the hash ahead of time and reheat it before serving. Whatever scenario you choose, this recipe will become a favorite to serve to company. Use vegetable broth to make this recipe gluten-free.

YOU WILL NEED

1 ½ pounds pork tenderloin, thin ends folded back and tied with kitchen twine

½ teaspoon kosher salt

½ teaspoon freshly ground black pepper

3 thick bacon slices, cut into 1-inch pieces

4 parsnips (about 1 pound), peeled and cut into ½-inch dice

1 Granny Smith apple, peeled, cored, and cut into ½-inch dice

1 tablespoon minced shallot

1 teaspoon minced fresh rosemary

SAUCE

¼ cup dry white vermouth or dry white wine

½ cup reduced-sodium chicken or vegetable broth

1 tablespoon cold unsalted butter

1 Preheat oven to 350°F. Season pork tenderloin with salt and pepper and let stand for 10 to 15 minutes.

2 Cook bacon in a large ovenproof skillet over medium heat, stirring occasionally, until crisp and browned, about 10 minutes. Using a slotted spoon, transfer to paper towels to drain. Pour off and reserve bacon fat.

3 Return 1 tablespoon of bacon fat to skillet and heat over medium heat. Add pork tenderloin and cook, turning occasionally, until browned on all sides, about 5 minutes. Transfer skillet to oven and bake, turning pork occasionally, until an instant-read thermometer inserted in center of tenderloin registers 145°F, 25 to 30 minutes.

continued

4 Bring a medium saucepan of lightly salted water to a boil over high heat. Add parsnips and cook just until barely tender, about 10 minutes. Drain, rinse under cold running water, and pat dry.

5 Heat 1 tablespoon of reserved bacon fat in a large skillet over medium heat. Add apple and cook, stirring occasionally, until beginning to brown, about 3 minutes. Add parsnips and cook, turning occasionally, until lightly browned, about 7 minutes. Add shallot and rosemary and cook until shallot softens, about 2 minutes more. Season with salt and pepper. Reduce heat to very low to keep warm.

6 Transfer tenderloin to a carving board and let stand for 5 minutes. Meanwhile, make sauce: Pour off any fat from skillet. Return skillet to high heat on stove. Pour in vermouth, then broth. Bring to a boil, scraping up any browned bits in skillet with a wooden spoon, and cook until reduced by half, about 3 minutes. Remove from heat, add butter, and whisk until butter is melted and lightly thickens sauce.

7 Remove strings and cut tenderloin crosswise into $1/2$-inch-thick slices. Stir bacon into hash. Serve tenderloin slices hot with hash, drizzled with sauce.

PORTOBELLO

CROQUE-MONSIEUR

MAIN COURSE

MAKES 1 SANDWICH

WINE SUGGESTION: BEAUJOLAIS

Here is a French member of the grilled cheese family, with a meaty portobello mushroom as its raison d'être. While portobello mushrooms are packed with flavor, their gills give off a good amount of inky juices. Use a tablespoon to scrape out the black gills from the underside of the mushroom cap, leaving the flavor but not the dark color.

YOU WILL NEED

1 portobello mushroom, stemmed and gills removed

1 teaspoon extra-virgin olive oil

Kosher salt and freshly ground black pepper

2 teaspoons unsalted butter

2 slices firm white sandwich bread

1 tablespoon Pesto (recipe follows)

1/3 cup (about 1 1/2 ounces) shredded Gruyère cheese

1 Heat oil in a medium nonstick skillet over medium heat. Add mushroom, flat side down, and cook until seared on bottom, about 4 minutes. Turn mushroom and cook until tender, about 2 minutes. Transfer to a plate and season mushroom with salt and pepper.

2 Wipe out skillet with moist paper towels. Add butter and melt over medium heat. Spread one bread slice with pesto and top with mushroom cap. Sprinkle with cheese and add second bread slice. Place sandwich in skillet. Cook, turning once, until golden brown on both sides, about 5 minutes. Serve hot.

PESTO: Pulse 3 tablespoons pine nuts or coarsely chopped walnuts and 1 chopped garlic clove in a food processor until minced. Add 2 cups packed fresh basil leaves, 1/2 cup freshly grated Parmigiano-Reggiano, and 1/4 cup packed fresh flat-leaf parsley leaves and pulse to chop herbs. With machine running, gradually add 1/2 cup extra-virgin olive oil to make a paste. Transfer to a container. Pour a little olive oil over back of a teaspoon to cover top of pesto completely with a thin layer of oil. Cover and refrigerate for up to 1 week or freeze for up to 2 months.

SAUSAGE &
RADICCHIO RISOTTO

RISOTTO

GF | 🍷

MAKES 4—6 SERVINGS

WINE SUGGESTION: VALPOLICELLA

Risotto is almost endlessly versatile. This version features radicchio's mildly bitter flavor, tempered by sweet sausage and creamy rice to create a memorable risotto. Cooking the maroon radicchio will tint the risotto a dull brown, but a topping of fresh radicchio brightens up the color and provides a textural contrast, as well. Use vegetable broth to make this recipe gluten-free.

YOU WILL NEED

2 heads radicchio (1 pound total)

3 cups reduced-sodium chicken or vegetable broth

3 cups water

2 tablespoons extra-virgin olive oil

1 pound sweet Italian pork or fresh turkey sausage, casings removed

1 yellow onion, chopped

2 garlic cloves, minced

1 1/2 cups (11 ounces) Arborio rice

1 cup dry white wine such as Pinot Grigio

1/2 cup (2 ounces) freshly grated Parmigiano-Reggiano

Kosher salt and freshly ground black pepper

1 Core radicchio and cut it crosswise into 1/8-inch shreds. You should have about 6 cups loosely packed radicchio; reserve about 1 1/2 cups to use as a garnish.

2 Bring broth and water to a boil in a medium saucepan over high heat. Turn heat to very low to keep broth hot.

3 Heat 1 tablespoon of oil in a large, heavy Dutch oven or saucepan over medium heat. Add sausage and cook, breaking up sausage with side of a spoon into small pieces, until it loses its pink color, about 5 minutes. Add onion and garlic and cook, stirring occasionally, until onion softens, about 3 minutes. Using a slotted spoon, transfer sausage mixture to a plate.

4 Add remaining 1 tablespoon oil to Dutch oven and heat. Add rice and cook, stirring often, until it turns opaque (do not brown), about 2 minutes. Return sausage mixture to pan. Add wine and cook until almost evaporated, about 2 minutes.

continued

5 Stir about 1 cup of hot broth mixture into rice. Cook, stirring almost constantly, until rice absorbs almost all of broth, about 3 minutes. Add another cup of broth and stir until it is almost absorbed. Repeat, keeping risotto at a steady simmer and adding more broth as it is absorbed, until you use all of stock and rice is barely tender, about 20 minutes total. If you run out of stock and rice isn't tender, use hot water. During last 5 minutes of cooking, stir in radicchio, in batches, until all but reserved 1 1/2 cups has been added and wilted.

6 Remove risotto from heat and stir in cheese. Season with salt and pepper. Spoon risotto into shallow soup bowls and top each serving with a mound of reserved radicchio.

FETTUCCINE WITH SHRIMP

& CREAMY LEMON SAUCE

PASTA

MAKES 4—6 SERVINGS

WINE SUGGESTION: PINOT GRIGIO

Rosemary, not a common herb with shrimp, cuts through the richness of this sauce. Because of the high cream content, you may want to serve it the Italian way, in small portions as a first course. Note that this recipe doesn't call for cheese, as there are some Italian regions that do not serve cheese with seafood. As we are not in Italy, feel free to add freshly grated Parmigiano-Reggiano if you wish.

YOU WILL NEED

2 tablespoons unsalted butter

1 pound large (21 to 25 count) shrimp, peeled and deveined

$^1/_3$ cup minced shallots

Grated zest of 1 large lemon

3 tablespoons fresh lemon juice (about 1 $^1/_2$ lemons)

2 cups heavy cream

$^3/_4$ cup reduced-sodium chicken broth

4 teaspoons minced fresh rosemary, plus small sprigs for garnish

Kosher salt and freshly ground black pepper

1 pound fettuccine

1 Melt 1 tablespoon of butter in a large skillet over medium-high heat. Add shrimp and cook, stirring occasionally, just until they turn opaque, about 2 minutes. Do not overcook shrimp, as they will be subjected to more heat later. Transfer shrimp to a plate.

2 Add remaining 1 tablespoon butter to skillet and melt. Add shallots and cook, stirring often, until softened. Add lemon zest and juice—juice will immediately evaporate into a glaze. Stir in cream, broth, and minced rosemary. Bring to a boil and cook until sauce has reduced to about 1 $^3/_4$ cups, 5 to 7 minutes. During last minute, return shrimp to skillet. Season sauce with salt and pepper.

3 Meanwhile, bring a large pot of lightly salted water to a boil over high heat. Add fettuccine and cook according to package directions until al dente. Drain well. Return fettuccine to pot. Add sauce to pasta and mix well. Serve hot in individual bowls, garnished with rosemary sprigs.

THREE-CHEESE
MACARONI & CHEESE

PASTA

MAKES 6 SERVINGS

It may seem like gilding the lily to add two more cheeses to the happy marriage of macaroni and Cheddar, but the interplay of flavors elevates this familiar dish to new heights. A touch of Dijon mustard also perks up the flavor. For an especially appetizing presentation, bake it in onion soup bowls or individual ovenproof crocks.

YOU WILL NEED

1 pound elbow macaroni

5 tablespoons unsalted butter

1/4 cup all-purpose flour

3 cups whole milk, heated

1 1/2 cups (6 ounces) shredded extra-sharp Cheddar cheese

1 1/2 cups (6 ounces) shredded Gruyère or Swiss cheese

2 teaspoons Dijon mustard

Salt

Red pepper sauce

1/2 cup (2 ounces) freshly grated Parmigiano-Reggiano

2 tablespoons dried bread crumbs

1 Preheat oven to 350°F. Lightly butter a deep 8-cup baking dish.

2 Bring a large pot of lightly salted water to a boil over high heat. Stir in macaroni. Cook until macaroni is almost but not quite tender (remember, it will bake in oven), about 8 minutes. Transfer macaroni to a colander and drain well.

3 Add 4 tablespoons of butter to pasta pot and melt over medium heat. Whisk in flour and reduce heat to low. Let bubble without browning for 2 minutes. Whisk in hot milk and cook, whisking often, until simmering and thickened. Remove from heat and whisk in Cheddar, Gruyère, and mustard. Return macaroni to pot and mix well. Season with salt and red pepper sauce. Spread in baking dish. Mix Parmigiano-Reggiano and bread crumbs and sprinkle over macaroni. Dot with remaining 1 tablespoon of butter.

4 Bake until macaroni is bubbling throughout, about 25 minutes. Let stand for 5 minutes, then serve hot.

ROASTED FINGERLING POTATOES
with CRÈME FRAÎCHE & HERBS

SIDE DISH

MAKES 6 SERVINGS

Fingerling potatoes are smaller and more elongated than the more common varieties, and should be cooked in their thin skins to show off their earthy colors. Toss them with buttery crème fraîche (or sour cream) and your favorite herbs (it's difficult to think of an herb that wouldn't go well here) to add interest to a simple roast potato side dish. Try this with grilled steak or roast beef.

YOU WILL NEED

2 tablespoons extra-virgin olive oil

2 pounds unpeeled fingerling potatoes, scrubbed and halved lengthwise

2 garlic cloves, thinly sliced

Kosher salt and freshly ground black pepper

½ cup crème fraîche or sour cream

2 tablespoons minced fresh chives

1 Preheat oven to 425°F. Spread 1 tablespoon of oil on a large rimmed baking sheet. Heat in oven until baking sheet is very hot but oil is not smoking, about 5 minutes.

2 In a large bowl, toss potatoes with remaining 1 tablespoon oil. Remove baking sheet from oven. Arrange potatoes, cut side down, on baking sheet. Bake until golden brown on bottom, about 30 minutes. Turn potatoes and bake 5 minutes more. Stir in garlic and cook until fragrant and softened but not browned, about 3 minutes.

3 Transfer potato mixture to a serving bowl and season with salt and pepper. Top with crème fraîche and chives and mix well. Serve at once.

POTATO & CARROT

PANCAKES

SIDE DISH

MAKES 4 SERVINGS

Hanukkah is the time for the potato pancakes called latkes. Golden brown, crisp and tender at the same time, they achieve their lightness thanks to the potato starch, gathered from the shredded potatoes, which holds them together without a lot of bread crumbs. Don't skimp on the oil, or the pancakes won't have that marvelous crunch.

 YOU WILL NEED

3 baking (russet) potatoes (1 1/4 pounds)

2 carrots, peeled

1 yellow onion

2 large eggs, beaten

2 tablespoons dried bread crumbs or matzo meal

1 teaspoon salt

1/4 teaspoon freshly ground black pepper

Vegetable oil, for frying

Sour cream and applesauce, for serving

1 Position a rack in center of oven and preheat oven to 200°F. Line a baking sheet with paper towels.

2 Peel potatoes, then shred them with a food processor fitted with a grating disk with large holes, or use large holes of a box grater. Working over a small bowl, squeeze potatoes to remove excess liquid and transfer potatoes to a large bowl. Set bowl of potato liquid aside for 5 minutes.

3 Shred carrots in food processor (using grating disk) and add to bowl with potatoes. Grate onion with same blade—it will be almost puréed—and add to potato mixture, discarding any large shreds of onion.

4 Carefully pour off all reddish potato liquid, leaving paste-like potato starch in bottom of bowl. Scrape starch into shredded vegetables. Add eggs, bread crumbs, salt, and pepper and mix well.

5 Pour $1/8$ inch oil into a large skillet and heat over medium-high heat until shimmering. Carefully add about $1/3$ cup batter for each pancake to oil, using bottom of cup to spread each into a 4-inch pancake. Cook until golden brown on bottom, about 3 minutes. Turn and brown on second side, about 3 more minutes. Using a slotted spatula, transfer to paper towels and keep warm in oven while making remaining pancakes. If needed, add more oil to skillet and heat before cooking second batch. Serve hot, with sour cream and applesauce.

MASHED TURNIPS

with **GARLIC**

SIDE DISH

GF | U

MAKES 4–6 SERVINGS

This dish is a full-flavored alternative to mashed potatoes, and is especially good with pork chops or roasts. Mellowed by potatoes and bolstered by garlic, the lowly turnip here becomes a very tasty side dish. Vegetable or chicken broth boosts the flavor, but you can use water alone, if you wish. Use vegetable broth (or water) to make this recipe gluten-free. While you should never use a food processor to mash plain potatoes, when they are mixed with a slightly larger amount of turnips, as in this recipe, you can purée them in a processor without fear.

YOU WILL NEED

1 ½ pounds turnips, peeled and cut into 1-inch chunks

1 pound baking (russet) potatoes, peeled and cut into 1-inch chunks

8 garlic cloves, crushed and peeled

1 ¾ cups reduced-sodium vegetable or chicken broth

Water as needed

3 tablespoons heavy cream or milk

2 tablespoons unsalted butter

Kosher salt and freshly ground black pepper

Chopped fresh flat-leaf parsley or dill, for serving

1 Combine turnips, potatoes, and garlic in a medium saucepan. Pour in broth and add just enough lightly salted cold water to barely cover vegetables. Bring to a boil over high heat. Reduce heat to medium, cover, and cook at a brisk simmer until vegetables are tender, about 25 minutes. Drain vegetables over a large heatproof bowl, reserving cooking liquid.

2 Purée vegetables with cream and butter in a food processor, adding reserved cooking liquid as desired. (For a coarser texture, mash with a hand masher or electric mixer and omit cooking water.) Season with salt and pepper. Transfer to a serving bowl and sprinkle with parsley. Serve hot.

CHOCOLATE-BANANA

CREAM PIE

Bananas are not grown as a commercial crop in this country, but the imported fruit provides a year-round source of natural sweetness. This makes them invaluable in the middle of winter when you want an over-the-top dessert like this one: homemade chocolate pudding layered over bananas in a chocolate cookie crust. It requires very little baking skill, but will guarantee raves.

YOU WILL NEED

CRUST

1 1/2 cups chocolate wafer or chocolate graham cracker crumbs

3 tablespoons unsalted butter, melted

1 tablespoon granulated sugar

FILLING

3 cups half-and-half

2/3 cup granulated sugar

1/8 teaspoon fine sea salt

1/4 cup cornstarch

4 large egg yolks

5 ounces bittersweet or semisweet chocolate, finely chopped

2 tablespoons unsalted butter

1 teaspoon vanilla extract

2 small bananas, peeled and cut into 1/4-inch-thick rounds

Whipped Cream (page 45)

Chocolate shavings (see note, page 185), for garnish (optional)

1 Preheat oven to 350°F. Lightly butter a 9-inch pie pan.

2 To make crust: Combine all crust ingredients in a medium bowl until evenly moistened. Press firmly and evenly over bottom and up sides of pan. Bake until crust is set, about 12 minutes. Transfer to a wire rack and let cool completely.

3 To make filling: Heat 2 1/2 cups of half-and-half with sugar and salt in a medium saucepan over medium heat, stirring often to dissolve sugar, until simmering. Remove from heat.

continued

4 Sprinkle cornstarch over remaining $1/2$ cup half-and-half in a small bowl and whisk until dissolved. Whisk egg yolks in a medium bowl and gradually whisk in cornstarch mixture. Gradually whisk in hot half-and-half mixture. Rinse out saucepan and return mixture to pan. Whisk over medium heat until mixture comes to a boil. Reduce heat to low and let bubble, whisking constantly, for 1 minute. Remove from heat and add chocolate, butter, and vanilla. Let stand for 3 minutes, then whisk until chocolate is completely melted.

5 Spread sliced bananas in bottom of cooled crust. Pour filling over bananas and smooth top. Press a sheet of plastic wrap directly on filling to keep a skin from forming. Let cool completely. Refrigerate until filling is chilled and set, at least 2 hours or overnight.

6 Spread the whipped cream over filling. (If you wish, transfer whipped cream to a pastry bag fitted with a star tip and pipe cream rosettes onto pie.) Garnish with chocolate shavings, if using. Slice and serve chilled.

CHOCOLATE SHAVINGS: Use a chunk of semisweet or bittersweet chocolate weighing at least 4 ounces. Let chocolate stand in a warm place for about 1 hour so surface is barely softened. (If too cold, the chocolate will break into shards.) Working over a sheet of waxed or parchment paper, use a swivel vegetable peeler to shave chocolate. Refrigerate for a few minutes to harden shavings. Do not touch shavings with your fingers when applying them to dessert or they will melt.

·POACHED PEARS·

in SPICED PORT SYRUP

DESSERT

MAKES 6 SERVINGS

WINE SUGGESTION: AGED PORT

Individual pears in a beautiful garnet-colored red wine syrup have become a winter dessert classic. Firm-ripe Bosc pears are the best choice, as they hold their shape well during cooking. You can buy mulling spices in The Fresh Market spice section, or make your own.

YOU WILL NEED

6 firm-ripe Bosc pears

1 lemon, halved

1 tablespoon mulling spices (see note)

One 750-ml bottle tawny or ruby port

1/3 cup packed light brown sugar

Vanilla ice cream, for serving

1 Peel pears, leaving stems intact. Rub exposed flesh with lemon halves. Choose a large nonreactive saucepan (stainless steel or enameled cast iron, but not uncoated aluminum or cast iron) just large enough to hold all of pears on their sides. Wrap mulling spices in a square of rinsed cheesecloth and tie into a packet with a piece of kitchen twine.

2 Bring port, brown sugar, and spice packet (without pears) to a simmer in saucepan over medium heat, stirring to dissolve sugar. Arrange pears on their sides in saucepan. Reduce heat to medium-low and cover tightly. Simmer, occasionally turning pears in syrup for even coloring, until pears are just tender when pierced with tip of a small, sharp knife, about 50 minutes. Using a slotted spoon, transfer to a shallow ceramic or glass baking dish.

3 Increase heat to high and bring port wine mixture to a boil. Cook until reduced to 1 cup, about 15 minutes. Discard spice packet. Pour syrup over pears and let cool. Cover tightly with plastic wrap. Refrigerate, occasionally turning pears in syrup, until chilled, at least 2 hours or up to 2 days.

4 Place each pear in a shallow soup bowl and divide syrup evenly over pears. Add a scoop of ice cream to each and serve at once, with spoons.

MULLING SPICE BLEND: Use one 2-inch cinnamon stick, 2 star anise pods, and 1/2 teaspoon *each* whole cloves, allspice berries, and dried orange peel.

INDEX

TABLE OF EQUIVALENTS

The exact equivalents in the following tables have been rounded for convenience.

LIQUID/DRY MEASURES

U.S.	METRIC
$1/4$ teaspoon	1.25 milliliters
$1/2$ teaspoon	2.5 milliliters
1 teaspoon	5 milliliters
1 tablespoon (3 teaspoons)	15 milliliters
1 fluid ounce (2 tablespoons)	30 milliliters
$1/4$ cup	60 milliliters
$1/3$ cup	80 milliliters
$1/2$ cup	120 milliliters
1 cup	240 milliliters
1 pint (2 cups)	480 milliliters
1 quart (4 cups, 32 ounces)	960 milliliters
1 gallon (4 quarts)	3.84 liters
1 ounce (by weight)	28 grams
1 pound	454 grams
2.2 pounds	1 kilogram

OVEN TEMPERATURE

FAHRENHEIT	CELSIUS	GAS
250	120	$1/2$
275	140	1
300	150	2
325	160	3
350	180	4
375	190	5
400	200	6
425	220	7
450	230	8
475	240	9
500	260	10

INGREDIENT SUBSTITUTIONS

With an emphasis on accessible, seasonal foods and healthful ingredients, many of the recipes in this book are well-suited for vegetarian, vegan, dairy-free, and gluten-free dietary considerations, as noted on the preceding pages. A quick glance at the Menu Builders on pages 8, 52, 106, and 144 as well as individual recipe pages shows which recipes meet these dietary categories. Occasionally, an easy ingredient substitution has been suggested to accommodate dietary preference.

You may decide to make further substitutions to enjoy certain recipes offered in this collection. For example, the Oven-Barbecued Country Ribs recipe on page 159 can be made using gluten-free ketchup and Worcestershire sauce, and Jambalaya the Big Easy Way on page 160 can be made using gluten-free spices, broth, tomatoes, and rice. You can find a variety of gluten-free products at The Fresh Market.